WASHINGTON, D.C.

WHITE HOUSE

The United States Presidents

Illustrated

Robert M. Reed

Schiffer Publishing Ltd

4880 Lower Valley Road · Atglen, PA · 19310

Other Schiffer Books by Robert M. Reed
Advertising Postcards. ISBN: 0-7643-1237-5. $29.95.
Christmas Postcards. ISBN: 978-0-7643-2689-9. $29.95.
Greetings From Indianapolis. ISBN: 978-0-7643-2629-5. $24.95.

"Old Glory" © John Hix. Image from BigStockPhoto.com.

Title Page: The White House, Undivided back postcard. Ca. 1905. $3-4.

Schiffer Books are available at special discounts for bulk purchases for sales promotions or premiums. Special editions, including personalized covers, corporate imprints, and excerpts can be created in large quantities for special needs. For more information contact the publisher:

Published by Schiffer Publishing Ltd.
4880 Lower Valley Road
Atglen, PA 19310
Phone: (610) 593-1777; Fax: (610) 593-2002
E-mail: Info@schifferbooks.com

For the largest selection of fine reference books on this and related subjects, please visit our web site at **www.schifferbooks.com**
We are always looking for people to write books on new and related subjects. If you have an idea for a book please contact us at the above address.

This book may be purchased from the publisher.
Include $5.00 for shipping.
Please try your bookstore first.
You may write for a free catalog.

In Europe, Schiffer books are distributed by
Bushwood Books
6 Marksbury Ave.
Kew Gardens
Surrey TW9 4JF England
Phone: 44 (0) 20 8392 8585; Fax: 44 (0) 20 8392 9876
E-mail: info@bushwoodbooks.co.uk
Website: www.bushwoodbooks.co.uk

Designed by RoS
Type set in Dutch 809 BT/Zurich BT
ISBN: 978-0-7643-3280-7
Printed in China

Contents

Book of Presidents.
1936 premium
booklet. $3-4.

Dedication

This book is dedicated to dear, sweet Rachel and the future.

Print of the White House. Published early 1890s. $10-15

White House, President's Office and Washington Monument

Acknowledgments

My deepest appreciation goes to Heather Reed, managing editor of Antique and Collectible News Service, who has contributed tirelessly to the editing, assembly, and completion of this volume.

Special appreciation also is felt for the following people: Marlo at Wierdcardsblogspot.com for lending some modern postcards; Janet James at the Woodrow Wilson Presidential Library; Dr. Elma Lee Moore, Dean of the School of Community Education at Wittenberg University; Amy Northup at the Franklin D. Roosevelt Presidential Library and Museum; Kristin Mooney at the Gerald R. Ford Presidential Library and Museum; Bonnie Blaford, park ranger for the National Park Service at Herbert Hoover National Historic Site; Martha Berryman, museum director at President Bill Clinton's First Home Museum Exhibit Center and Museum Store; John Powell, curator of Woodrow Wilson House in Washington, D.C.; Carrie Kibby at the McKinley Memorial Library; Christian Goos at the Gerald R. Ford Presidential Library; Pam Hinkhouse at the Hoover Library-Museum; Carol Kay Johnson at the President Lyndon Johnson Library and Museum; Dennis Latta at the William H. Harrison Mansion; Melissa Wood at the Mount Vernon George Washington Mansion; and the world-class auctioneers and appraisers at Skinner Inc.

Stand By The President. Early 1900s. $3-4.

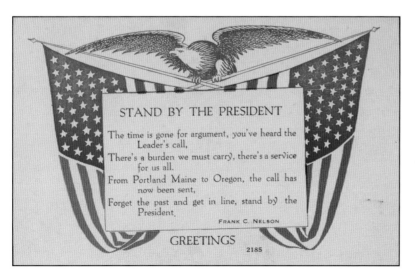

STAND BY THE PRESIDENT

The time is gone for argument, you've heard the
  Leader's call,
There's a burden we must carry, there's a service
  for us all.
From Portland Maine to Oregon, the call has
  now been sent,
Forget the past and get in line, stand by the
  President.

FRANK C. NELSON

GREETINGS
2185

Introduction

When I was four years old my mother left me alone in our upstairs apartment. It was only briefly while she went to the corner grocery store a little more than half-a-block away.

I would pass the time listening intently to the radio. At that time in the afternoon my world revolved around The Tom Mix Ralston Straight Shooters. Each weekday the cowboy good guys fought the bad guys. Each time the good guys won.

It was raining outside but I scarcely noticed as the radio sounds filled my head.

Then, in the midst of it all, something strange happened. The radio drama abruptly stopped. The somber voice of a radio announcer said he regretted to announce that President Franklin Roosevelt had died.

The announcer slowly repeated the same statement. The President had died.

As the radio began playing mournful music, I dashed for the closet.

My Mother's ironclad rule was to never leave the apartment unless it was an emergency. As I quickly donned my bright yellow raincoat I figured this was an emergency. The President had died.

The other ironclad rule my Mother had instilled in me was that even in an emergency I was to go no further than the iron fence post at the edge of the sidewalk. I could wait there in a true emergency—but go no further.

I waited silently in the rain until I could see my Mother coming down the sidewalk towards me.

"Bobby," she exclaimed, "what on earth are you doing out here in the rain?"

"The President has died," I stammered.

"Now Bobby, it was probably just the radio show that you heard. They—"

"No, no," I gasped, "the man on the radio said it. It was real."

And so it was real.

The President of the United States had died.

When my dear Mother realized that her little messenger was very accurate and maybe a little brave for bearing such awesome news, she hugged me and kissed my cheek. She even rewarded me later with a home-baked cookie.

As I went to sleep that night I could not help feeling that possibly the most important person in the world had died.

After all those years I still remember that day.

And, at times, I think I can still remember the taste of that wonderful cookie.

From childhood to adulthood the concept remains that presidents are important people; perhaps even some of the most important people in the world. Their actions and inactions become history. Countless lives are changed, altered, or ended as a result of presidential judgment. Often their influence on events continue long after they leave the power and pomp of the presidency. Sometimes it did not.

Some American presidents we know better than others. Some we wish we could sit down with today and chat about their days in the White House. This book explores those ideas.

There are at least two things these American presidents have in common. One will be forever compelling. The other might just be incidental. Number one is that each of them—every single one—came from our midst. They too had been more or less ordinary citizens. "We draw our presidents from the people," President Calvin Coolidge once said. "It is a wholesome thing for them to return to the people. I came from them. I wish to be one of them again." Another thing these American presidents had in common was that sooner or later they appeared on a postcard or two. George Washington and Abraham Lincoln were featured on virtually hundreds of different postcards over the years. Franklin Pierce and Chester Arthur have appeared on considerably less. Further, what some would call the modern presidents—being those who have been elected in the past 20 years or so—have not been so flattered with their image on postcards simply because the use of the postcard as a medium has dwindled considerably.

Taken on the whole, the American presidents and illustrations in which they appear convey history and become a fascinating and worthwhile study. To that end they are presented here.

George Washington

President 1789 - 1797

America's first president, George Washington, remains history's only unanimous choice for President. History records that Washington garnered one vote each from all 69 participating electors. Electors casting 'second choice' votes were divided. The most, 34, went to John Adams making him the country's very first vice-president.

While George Washington's birthday has long been celebrated on February 22, he was technically born on February 11, 1731. As a youngster he celebrated his birthday on the latter date. However in 1750 the British Parliament changed the type of calendar used. The jumbled result added 11 days to the 'new' Gregorian calendar giving Washington a revised birthday of February 22.

The father of the future president was Augustine Washington. Augustine fathered ten children in all, four by his first wife and six by his second wife. George was his fifth child but the very first given birth by second wife Mary Ball Washington.

Augustine died when young George was but 11 years old. Washington then went to live with a half-brother Lawrence, who built Mount Vernon. Washington was said to have a keen ability in mathematics and an attraction for the out doors. The two factors apparently led to an early interest in surveying land. As a teenager he was earning money as an apprentice surveyor.

Washington first served in the military in 1753 under the command of the Governor of Virginia. Back once again in civilian life he was married in 1759 to Martha Dandridge Custis, a widow. The two made their home at Mount Vernon where Washington maintained the large land holdings inherited from his step-brother's estate.

When the American Revolutionary loomed Washington eventually became commander-in-chief of the American army. General Washington commanded for seven long years staving up British forces in a series of up and down military encounters. A staunch supporter of a concept of an independent but powerful country, Washington called for a Constitutional Convention immediately after the British surrender.

During the writing of the U.S. Constitution at the Constitutional Convention in 1787 in Philadelphia, Washington served as chairman of the convention. Once the Constitution was completed the next step for the young nation would be to elect a president.

The election of 1789 was late getting underway. It had first been set for March 4 of that year in New York City's Federal Hall. However due to weather and various other delays it did not occur until more than a month later. As there were no true political parties at the time, each elector could vote for two persons—basically a first choice and a second choice. Washington won the election by winning all the first choice votes.

President George Washington took that first oath of office outside of the Federal Hall there in New York. Shortly afterwards he delivered his inaugural address in the Senate Chamber.

Initially Washington lived at Number 1 Cherry Street in New York City. Technically it was not the presidential mansion, but simply the Washington residence. In the early years of this country living quarters were not provided for the President by the federal government.

When Washington was elected to a second term he took the oath of office in Philadelphia. American's second president John Adams was also inaugurated in Philadelphia.

"As the first of everything, in our situation will serve to establish a precedent," Washington once wrote to James Madison, "it is devoutly wished on my part that these precedents mat be fixed on true principles."

Washington served two full terms but declined a third term in the belief that two terms were enough for any one president. That Washington precedent remained in place until 1940 when Franklin D. Roosevelt was elected for a third term. Later the U.S. Constitution was changed limiting all future presidents to no more than two full terms.

The first president died at Mount Vernon on December 14, 1799 after less than three years in retirement. He was buried there in the family vault. The nation was in mourning for months afterward.

In the mind's eye of America, President Washington is seen as he was depicted in the famed portrait by artist Gilbert Stuart. That remarkable portrait was one of the few objects originally put in the White House in 1800. It was one of the few objects saved by First Lady Dolley Madison when she fled the British invasion of Washington, D.C. in 1814.

Presidential Site:
Mount Vernon George Washington Mansion, Mount Vernon, Virginia, 703-780-2000

Postcard of Gilbert Stuart portrait. Cincinnati Art Museum. $2-3.

Postcard of Thomas Sully painting. Washington Crossing Card Collectors Club. $2-3.

Washington hatchet. Early 1900s. $6-8

Washington's Birthday. Early 1900s. $6-8

Washington. Early 1900s. $5-6

Washington at Yorktown. Posted 1910. $10-12

George Washington. Engraved print, copyright 1901 Gravure Company of America. $6-8.

Washington crossing the Delaware. Early 1900s. $6-8

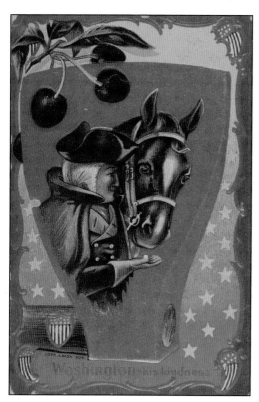

Washington- his kindness. Posted 1910. $6-8

Three Cheers for George. Early 1900s. $6-8

My Patriotic Greetings. Copyright 1909. $6-8

Washington in private life. Early 1900s. $6-8

Postcard of portrait. Early 1900s. $4-5

Here's to the Birthday. Early 1900s. $4-5

Battle of Trenton. Early 1900s. $4-5

George and Martha Washington. Ca. 1938. $3-4

Washington, his truthfulness. Copyright 1909. $6-8

Mount Vernon. Posted 1967. $2-3

The President's House. Posted 1914. $6-8

Washington bedroom, Mt. Vernon. Ca. 1950s. $2-3

Washington's Mount Vernon. Early 1900s. $2-3

Washington's Headquarters. Early 1900s. $2-3

Washington Monument, Philadelphia. Posted 1905. $3-5

His candor.... Posted 1913. $6-8

The Washington Tomb. Ca. 1960s. $2-3

Washington's Valley Forge office. Early 1900s. $2-3

John Adams

President 1797 - 1801

John Adams, our nation's second president, was the first vice president in history to be then elected as president.

Adams had previously impacted the founding of the country. In advancing the cause of freedom he helped to draft the Declaration of Independence.

This would be president was born October 30, 1735 in a place now known as Quincy, Massachusetts. The actual birth took place in a 'salt box' style home which was typical of homes built by New England farmers during the Colonial period. The cottage, one of two on the site, is the oldest presidential birthplace in the United States. It was frequently featured on postcards during the 20th century.

Later one of the two 'salt box' homes would also be the site of the birth of Adams' son John Quincy Adams who would also someday become president.

In October of 1764 Adams married 19-year old Abigail Smith. Later in his career Abigail would sometimes be referred to as Mrs. President because of her seemingly major influence on the presidency. The feisty Mrs. Adams, history suggests, often chided her husband about the lack of opportunities for women. Her letters to President Adams, while they were apart, sometimes pointedly made reference to what would centuries later be known as women's issues.

Early on Adams worked well with Thomas Jefferson in their noble effort to mold the government of the young country. However in the early days of the administration of President George Washington they became at odds. Adams as vice-president sought to move in one direction while Jefferson as Secretary of State favored another direction.

By the time Washington left office, Jefferson sternly wrote, "The President is fortunate to get off just as the bubble is bursting, leaving others to hold the bag."

Washington had indeed declined to serve a third four-year term in 1796. Consequently a group of strong central government Federalists supported vice president Adams for the top job. Meanwhile a group of anti-Federalist leaders and lawmakers, known as Democrat-Republicans supported Jefferson.

In those days presidential electors were selected in various ways depending upon which particular state was involved. That historic year 16 states participated and Adams got 71 elector votes compared to 68 for Jefferson. Under then prevailing rules Adams was elected president, and Jefferson in second place became vice president. Lots of other candidates got votes that year including two for Washington who was, of course, not a candidate.

The situation was further complicated by the fact that Adams and Jefferson were technically from two different political parties. Today such a configuration would not be possible. It 1797 it was perfectly permissible.

Adams became president in March of 1797. He took office in Philadelphia where the nation's government was then located.

Ironically by the time Adams actually did move into the 'President's House' in Washington, D.C. he was practically being given an eviction notice by the electorate.

Adams had sought a second term in 1800. However the Republican-Democrats this time were united and well organized. Federalists men were seriously divided and disorganized. As a result Jefferson defeated Adams by a margin of eight electoral votes.

The loss was a bitter one for President Adams. He refused to attend the inauguration ceremonies of his winning rival Jefferson.

After a stinging defeat Adams retired to his farm in Massachusetts. He and his wife took up residence in a mansion then known as Old House. The home is now a national historic site.

In their latter years Adams and Jefferson rekindled their friendship through a prolonged correspondence. Jefferson would call the constant exchange of letters, "the affections of the most cordial moments of our lives."

John Adams died on July 4, 1826. His last words were said to have been, "Jefferson survives." Oddly he was in error as Thomas Jefferson had himself died a few hours earlier.

The day of Adams death marked the 50th anniversary of the Declaration of Independence. Adams was 91.

Presidential Site:
Adams National Historic Site, Quincy, Massachusetts, 617-773-1177

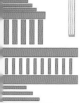

John Adams. Engraved print. Copyright 1901, The Gravure Company of America. $8-12

Birthplace of John Adams. Ca. 1930s. $2-3

Postcard based on drawing. Mrs. Abigail Smith Adams. $3-4

Postcard based on drawing. President John Adams. $3-4

John Adams

President John Adams. Colonial Bread premium card. 1976. $2-3

John Adams, second president. Real photo postcard. $5-6

Postcard based on oil painting. By Morris Katz. 1967. $3-4

Thomas Jefferson

President 1801 - 1809

Of all the American presidents, President Thomas Jefferson may have been the most talented.

Jefferson's accomplishments extended from architect to writer. Further he was an accomplished musician, statesman, and inventor. And then there was the Declaration of Independence thing, of which Jefferson was the leading author.

About the only skill Jefferson did not have was one of public speaking. Consequently he honed his writing skills with articles and volumes of letters rather than speeches. He was naturally one of the most articulate pens on paper of the Colonial era.

Thomas Jefferson was born April 13, 1743 in Albemarle County, Virginia. He was third of ten children born to a fairly well-to-do family. At the time the Virginia frontier was under rule of the British Empire.

He attended college at William and Mary, and later studied law. At age 26 he was first elected to the Virginia Legislature. Two years later he married Martha Wayles Skelton and took her to the mountain top home of Monticello which was still under construction.

Monticello became a showplace. The 35-room mansion, built by slaves who crafted even the bricks themselves, remains an historic landmark.

Jefferson's personal life was tragic. His wife died ten years after their marriage. As she lay dying he promised her he would never marry and he never did. He entered the White House nearly two decades later as a widower.

Politically however he was highly successful. He eventually became governor of Virginia, Minister to France, and late Secretary of State under President George Washington. In 1796 Jefferson was a candidate for president, and came within three votes of victory in the Electoral College. Under laws of that time the candidate in second place became vice president. Thus Jefferson became vice president in the administration of President John Adams, even though they were generally at odds politically.

Jefferson was a presidential candidate for the second time in 1800. That year Jefferson and Aaron Burr each ended by with 73 votes and a tie for first place in the Electoral College. Oddly both Jefferson and Burr were members of the Democrat-Republican Party whereas John Adams had been a member of the Federalist Party.

The tie-vote was then decided in the House of Representatives. After 36 ballots and much deliberation, Jefferson emerged as President of the United States.

While Jefferson was the third president he was the first to take the oath of office in Washington, D.C. Historic accounts say March 4, 1801 was a fair day and Jefferson walked to the Capitol from Mrs. Conrad's board house just over a block away. The oath was administered by Chief Justice John Marshall in the Senate Chamber of the Capitol. The center of the Capitol building itself was unfinished, only the north wing of the building had been completed.

Outgoing President John Adams had rushed out of the city by carriage at dawn, refusing to attend the inauguration of his successor. Adams had been very vocal in his feelings that the country would go to ruin in the hands of Jefferson.

During the Jefferson administration the Louisiana Purchase was completed. For roughly $11 million dollars the land territory of the United States was nearly doubled to 846,000 miles.

Jefferson served for two terms as president, believing that no person should prevail in the White House for more terms than that. He retired seemingly without regret to live in his Monticello home. There he spent much of the rest of his life writing and receiving letters from friends and acquaintances. Upon his death executors found 26,000 letters and 16,000 copies of his answers in his meticulous files.

The line from one private letter Jefferson wrote is emblazed upon the Thomas Jefferson National Memorial in Washington, D.C. It reads:

"I have sworn upon the altar of God eternal hostility against every form of tyranny over the mind of man."

President Jefferson died on the same day as President John Adams, July 4, 1826. The date was exactly 50 years to the day after the signing of the Declaration of Independence.

Centuries later President John F. Kennedy acknowledged the remarkable talent of the man from Monticello with this quote. While hosting a dinner of 49 Noble Prize winners, Kennedy told the group:

"I think this is the most extraordinary collection of talent and human knowledge that has ever been gathered at the White House, with the possible exception of when Thomas Jefferson dined alone."

Presidential Site:

Thomas Jefferson Memorial Foundation, Charlottesville, Virginia, 434-984-9800

Thomas Jefferson. Copyright 1901, The Gravure Company of America. $8-12

Thomas Jefferson, third president. Real photo postcard. $5-6

Thomas Jefferson

THIRD PRESIDENT 1801-1809
BORN-1743   DIED-1826

P-03 BECK

Monticello and Jefferson. Real photo postcard. $1-3

Thomas Jefferson. Whitman Publishing Co. postcard. $1-3

Thomas Jefferson statue. Posted 1960. $2-3

Thomas Jefferson. American Historical Prints postcards. $3-4

Thomas Jefferson and daughter. Real photo postcard. $3-4

Monticello. Ca. 1950s. $2-3

Jefferson carriage. Early 20th century. $1-3

Thomas Jefferson grave. Early 20th century. $2-3

James Madison

President 1809 - 1817

President James Madison was a giant among those framing the American constitution, but physically he was the smallest president to serve in the White House.

Madison stood only five feet and four inches tall and weighed a mere hundred pounds. Despite his record small stature, he was the only president—before or since—to have led troops under enemy fire while still holding the office of president.

The fourth president of the United States was the first to have been a Member of Congress. He was also the first to be younger than either of two vice-presidents serving with him. Both vice-presidents died while in office.

James Madison was born March 16 of 1751 in Port Conway, Virginia. As a youngster he was the oldest of twelve children and generally sickly. Partly because his ill health kept him physically inactive, he became an ardent student and scholar. After graduation from Princeton University he became a lawyer. In 1776, a very exciting time for this country, Madison became a delegate to the Williamsburg convention that declared independence for Virginia and established a state government.

The future president was elected to the House of Representatives in 1789 directly helping enact the first 10 amendments to the U.S. Constitution, which are now known as the Bill of Rights.

Cupid's arrow found Madison in 1794 when he married a 26-year old widow named Dorothea Payne. As a bride, she was quite a bit younger than the 43-year-old groom but proved to be a grand companion. To friends and loved ones and new Mrs. Madison was fondly known as Dolley, although historians have sometimes mistakenly spelled it out as simply Dolly.

Through the 1790s Madison labored mightily to refine the framework of the American government warning urgently that "censorial power" should be in the people over government and not in the government over people.

Sometimes Madison was applauded as the "Father of the Constitution." However just as often as he stressed the document was the work of many people, or as he phrased it, "many heads and many hands."

In 1801 Madison was appointed Secretary of State by then President Thomas Jefferson. Moreover he became a very close personal advisor to President Jefferson as well. Interestingly Dolley Madison too joined the Jefferson administration by serving as White House hostess since Jefferson was widowed.

After serving two terms as president Jefferson made the same decision that George Washington had made before him, not to seek a third term. Historians disagree, but it seems likely that Madison was Jefferson's choice to succeed him. At any rate in 1808 the Democratic-Republican party caucus chose Madison as their presidential candidate.

That year his opponent nominated by the Federalist party was Charles Pinckney of South Carolina. Madison was swept into office with nearly 70 percent of the electoral votes.

Madison was inaugurated into the presidency at age 57. When he moved into the White House the new First Lady was right at home.

"Whatever Madison's deficiencies in charm, his buxom wife Dolley compensated for them with her warmth and gaiety," wrote historian Frank Freidel in his book, Our Country's Presidents, "she was the toast of Washington."

Ultimately President Madison served his country through two terms and one war. During his second term of office a confrontation with the British erupted into a major conflict. In reaction to the British seizing of American sailors and cargo, Madison asked Congress for a declaration of war in the summer of 1812. The young country however was ill prepared for such a war with a world power and the British easily prevailed.

At one point nearly two years later the enemy invaded the city of Washington and Madison himself briefly led a skirmish against the British invasion. Ultimately Madison and the American troops were forced to flee. Dolley Madison was credited with saving the Declaration of Independence and a portrait of President Washington before she herself was forced to flee. The approaching British were able to set fire to the White House and part of the Capitol building before returning to the shore.

Just a month later the British were considerably less successful when they attacked Fort McHenry near Baltimore. They were repelled by American forces in a terrific battle which inspired Frances Scott Key to write The Star Spangled Banner, the national anthem.

Eventually the U.S. and the British ended the war with a treaty initiated by Madison in 1814, and an era of peace and prosperity prevailed. One political repercussion of it all was the demise of the Federalist party which had generally opposed the war and had specifically opposed President Madison.

After two terms, Madison, like Jefferson and Washington before him-- declined to seek a third term. He retired to his 5,000 acre farm near the home of Jefferson in Montpelier, Virginia.

The former president lived graciously and actively for the next 20 years. He took daily walks and is even said to have run foot races with the former First Lady. He died in 1836 at age 85.

A diminutive President, Madison remains the smallest person to hold that position. That record is likely to stand no matter what the gender of any future president. Hillary Clinton, for example, at 5 foot six inches and 120 to 130 pounds would have towered over James Madison.

Presidential Sites:

James Madison Museum, Orange, Virginia, 703-672-1776

James Madison's Montpelier, Montpelier Station, Virginia, 703-672-2728

Postcard based on Morris Katz portrait. Dated 1987. $3-4

James Madison

FOURTH PRESIDENT 1809-1817
BORN-1751   **DIED-1836**

P-04 BECK

James Madison, fourth president. Real photo postcard. $5-6

President and Mrs. James Madison

President and Mrs. Madison. Real photo postcard. $2-3

Birthplace marker. Real photo postcard. $2-3

President James Madison. Colonial Bread premium. Dated 1976. $2-3

James Madison. Engraved print; copyright 1901 The Gravure Company of America. $4-6

James Monroe

President 1817 - 1825

President James Monroe, the fifth person to hold that high office, was the first president to have been a United States Senator.

Monroe who took office in 1817 had not only been a young soldier in the American Revolutionary War but he had been shot in the shoulder while serving with the 3rd Virginia Regiment. He carried the bullet in his body through the rest of his life.

Historians identify Monroe as the soldier carrying the American flag in the famous painting of George Washington Crossing the Delaware.

The future president was born April 28, 1758 in Westmoreland County, Virginia. At age 17, the oldest of five children, Monroe enlisted as an American soldier in the war of independence. Later he married Elizabeth Kortright, and went on to serve as governor of Virginia. He eventually was elected U.S. Senator from that state.

Monroe's presidential ambitions surfaced as early as 1808 when he briefly sought to run against James Madison. Despite being unsuccessful Monroe won favor with President Madison and in 1811 he was appointed Secretary State. The following year Monroe was appointed Secretary of War. Ultimately he would become the first president to have held two cabinet posts.

By 1816 Monroe had Madison's full support in his bid for the presidential nomination within the caucus of the Republican-Democrat party. Others leaned toward William Harris Crawford for the nomination. In the end Monroe gained the nomination by a vote of 65 to 54. The Federalists meanwhile supported Rufus King of New York. During the general election of 1816 Monroe won handily with 84 percent of the electoral vote.

The new president became the first in history to take the oath of office outside instead of inside the confines of the Capitol Building. The move was prompted by fears that the floor of the hall of Congress might collapse under the weight of the expected crowd. The alternative was a ceremony on a raised portico outside of the mighty building. It was a practice that continued almost without exception into the 21st century.

In a final fashion statement President Monroe became the last president to be wearing knee breeches during his inaugural. Regular pants would be the rule with subsequent presidents.

Most all accounts indicate Monroe's first four-year term in office went exceptionally well. The pro-Federalist Columbian Centinel in Boston proclaimed, "an era of good feelings," and that slogan caught-on to the extent that it is still used in history books today.

During his relatively peaceful first term in office construction was begun on the Erie Canal, and Illinois became the first of six states that would be admitted to the Union during his tenure.

When the 1820 election rolled around President Monroe received nearly every single electoral vote. The lone exception was an elector who maintained that only George Washington had been deserving of the unanimous number of electoral votes.

During Monroe's second term in office the legendary Monroe Doctrine was proclaimed. It basically declared that any untoward act upon a nation in the Western Hemisphere would be seen as hostile to the United States as well.

Monroe managed to enjoy still another 'first' during his terms as president. His daughter Maria Hester Monroe, became the first daughter to be wed in the White House.

If President Monroe's career had a downside it developed as he left office. When he retired in 1826 he was faced with considerable personal debt. Eventually he was forced to sell his grand home in Virginia. The home—at various times known as Highlands, Ashfield, and Ashlawn—stood majestically near the home of Thomas Jefferson.

Accounts vary regarding the circumstances surrounding the death of President Monroe. Some say he was merely visiting his daughter in New York City when in died in 1831. Others say he was actually living there nearly impoverished by debts he owed.

At the time of his death he became the third president to die on the Fourth of July holiday. Both John Adams and Thomas had died five years earlier on July 4th.

Monroe was buried at Hollywood Cemetery in Richmond, Virginia.

Presidential Sites:
Ash Lawn-Highland Home of James Monroe, Charlottesville, Virginia, 434-293-9539
James Monroe Museum and Memorial Library, Fredericksburg, Virginia 540-654-1043

James Monroe. Engraved print; copyright
1901 The Gravure Company of America. $5-6

Monroe Law Office and Garden. Ca. 1930s. $2-3

President and Mrs. Monroe. Real photo postcard. $3-4

Statue of James Monroe. Real photo
postcard. Ca. 1940s. $4-5

Ash Lawn, Home of President Monroe. Ca. 1930s. $3-4

Boxwood Hedges at Ash Lawn. Ca. 1940s. $2-3

Postcard depicting Monroe bust by Margaret Cresson. Law Office Museum and Library. Ca. 1960s. $2-3

James Monroe, Fifth President. James Monroe Shrine postcard. $6-8

Postcard based on Morris Katz portrait. Dated 1987. $3-4

23

John Quincy Adams

President 1825 - 1829

President John Quincy Adams was a person who truly followed in his father's footsteps.

Like his father he was born in one of two houses sitting side by side. Like his father he graduated from Harvard. Like his father he became a foreign diplomat. And like his father, he eventually became president of the United States.

At the time, long before George H. and George W. Bush, the presidents Adams were the first father and son combination.

John Quincy Adams was born July 11, 1767 in Braintree, Massachusetts. He was the second child in a family of five.

Some accounts say a young John Quincy witnessed history as he and his mother Abigail Adams watched the Battle of Bunker Hill from a hill above the family farm. He was well educated, graduated from Harvard University, and was soon serving his country in other countries.

Adams was far enough in his foreign service career to become Secretary of State under President James Monroe. In 1820 Adams oddly ended with one single electoral vote for president. His former boss, President Monroe garnered all the rest.

In the presidential election of 1824 Adams was a much more earnest participant. As it turned out he was one of four candidates representing the Democrat-Republican Party. The others were Andrew Jackson, William Crawford, and Henry Clay. After a fierce campaign the results were as follows: Jackson had 153,544 votes and 99 electoral votes; Adams had 108,740 popular votes and 84 electoral votes; Crawford had 42 electoral votes; and Clay had 37 electoral votes.

Since no candidate had the required majority (just a plurality) the contest went to the House of Representatives. Clay, apparently wishing to thwart the candidacy of rival Jackson, released his votes to Adams making Adams the winner. Jackson was furious, but Adams and Clay became allied as National Republicans. Later their group became part of the Whig Party.

The dramatic unfolding of events made Adams the first president to be elected without a true majority of the votes.

At the March 4, 1825 swearing-in ceremony Adams was in one carriage which was followed up Capitol Hill by the outgoing president in another carriage. The actual event took place in the House Chamber of the restored Capitol. Ironically it would be the same place where Adams would die many years later.

Although Adams entered the White House somewhat optimistically in hopes things would go swimmingly, it was not to be. Soon he was frustrated with opposition from Jackson and his allies in Congress. Some scholars had credited the 'Washington frustration' for Adams' rigid schedule.

Typically Adams rose at four or five in the morning, built his own fire, read his Bible, wrote in his diary, and took a long walk. At times the walks included an early morning swim in the Potomac River. All before the White House staff was up and about.

During the day he had the loving companionship of First Lady Louisa Catherine Adams. Louisa was born in England the daughter of United States Consul Joshua Johnson. John and Louisa were married in England (the first president to wed outside of the U.S.) when she was only 22. They lived there for four years before they sailed for America and she saw the country for the first time.

Some accounts said John Quincy Adams was with the family at the White House for the traditional Fourth of July public reception on 1826 when he learned of the death of two presidents. He first learned of the death of President Thomas Jefferson. Next he was informed of the death of his own father, President John Adams. Both of these past presidents were signers of the Declaration of Independence.

Adams' apparent fondness of billiards caused a political flap during his administration. At some point Adams had listed a $50 billiard table, $5 cues, and $6 worth of billiard balls as official White House expenses. When some members of Congress loudly complained, Adams paid for the items himself.

Despite a growing number of political losses, Adams was able to help ensure the successful establishment of the Smithsonian Institution in Washington, D.C.

The nation's sixth president sought re-election but was defeated by old rival Andrew Jackson. Like his father before him, John Quincy Adams served only a single term.

"No one knows, and few conceive, the agony of mind that I have suffered," he would later write in his diary, "from the time I was made by circumstances, and not by my volition, a candidate for the presidency till I was dismissed from that station by failure of my re-election...."

Stinging from the defeat Adams refused to attend the inauguration of President Jackson early in 1829.

In 1831 he again became a member of Congress and served for 17 years. In 1848 in collapsed on the floor of the House from a stroke. He was moved to the Speaker's Room where he died two days later.

"America has lost a man who loved her with heart," wrote a fellow citizen at his passing, "religion lost a supporter; freedom lost an unfailing friend; and mankind a noble vindicator or our inalienable rights."

Adams was buried where his father and mother lay at First Parish Church in Quincy, Massachusetts. Later his wife Louisa was also buried there.

Presidential Site:
Adams National Historic Site, Quincy, Virginia,
617-773-1177

John Quincy Adams (1767 - 1848)

Postcard based on portrait by John Copley.
Real photo postcard. $4-5

Ca. 19th century. $4-5

GARDEN—Adams Mansion—Home of Two Presidents—135 Adams St., Quincy, Mass.

Home of Two Presidents. Ca. 1930s. $2-3

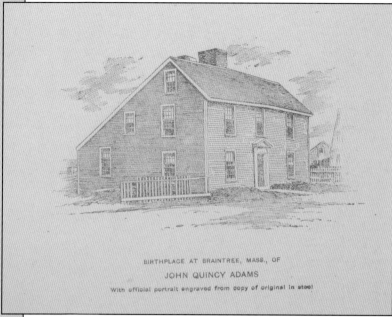

Ca. 19th century. $4-5

Engraved print of J. Q. Adams from official portrait. Copyright 1901, The Gravure Company of America. $8-10

President and Mrs. Adams. Real photo postcard. $3-4

Birthplaces of John and John Quincy Adams. Dated 1964. $2-3

Andrew Jackson

President 1829 - 1837

Postcards came of age, of course, long after the terms of President Andrew Jackson. However Jackson was later memorialized on various postcards depicting him, his wife, and his beloved Hermitage home.

The feisty President Jackson is probably better known to younger generations today for his image on the $20 dollar bill. The seventh president of the United States was once better known for fighting duels and twice marrying a divorced woman.

America's lanky six-foot, 145 pound frontier president was actually born in a log cabin. Jackson's father, a farmer, died before Andrew was born in 1767. His mother died when Jackson was only 14 years old, but he had already joined the army.

Largely self-educated, Old Hickory eventually became a lawyer in Nashville, Tennessee. He was much more famous however as a general and a war hero during the War of 1812. Jackson is credited with leading American troops to victory against the British in the Battle of New Orleans.

Jackson fell in love with a woman named Rachel Donelson Robards. The two were married in 1790 in Natchez, Mississippi. However the situation was complicated. Rachel had been previously married to Captain Lewis Robards. Earlier in 1790 she was granted the right to sue for divorce by the Virginia legislature.

She assumed the act had granted a divorce. In reality it had only granted the right to continue with the legal procedure. In 1794 after the final divorce decree was finally served on Captain Robards, Rachel and Andrew were again married. This time the wedding was held in Nashville, Tennessee.

Historically Jackson became the only American president to marry the same woman twice. He was also the first U.S. President to marry a divorced woman.

Jackson, according to many accounts, was prone to be hot-tempered and was always ready to challenge opponents to a duel. Some historians suggest Jackson participated in as many as 100 of them.

At least one duel may have involved the fair name of his wife. Reportedly he challenged Charles Dickenson in 1806 after Dickenson was said to have made unkind comments about Mrs. Jackson and her previous marriage. Dickenson fired first wounding Jackson. The future president fired his .70 caliber bullet true fatally injuring Dickenson.

Still another account suggests Jackson challenged Tennessee governor John Sevier to a duel for similar wifely slander. This time, in the Jackson-Sevier encounter, there were no injuries.

In regard to politics, Jackson ultimately belonged to a faction of the Democrat-Republican party, which came to be known as the Democrat party. His rival, John Quincy Adams, was a member of a faction of the same group known as the National Republican Party. It would later be known as the Whig party.

Despite his antics, Jackson was very popular with the people at the time of the presidential election in 1828. He and his running mate John Calhoun won handily over Adams and Richard Rush.

Tragically Jackson's wife, Rachel, died of a heart attack in December of 1828. When he took the oath of office the following March he was a widower.

During his term in the White House he became the first president to ride on the railroad. Jackson sought re-election in 1832, and it was the first time candidates were nominated by national conventions rather than legislative bodies. Jackson's vice presidential candidate was Martin Van Buren. The two defeated Republicans Henry Clay and John Sergeant.

Given the times, many historians suggest Jackson could have sought and won a third term as president. At the time there was no law or amendment prohibiting such a run; however Jackson declined and pledged his support to Van Buren.

President Jackson retired to his 425 acre estate The Hermitage. Located not far from Nashville, the grounds had been purchased in 1804 and was the site of numerous homes. The main home, built in 1818, became a major tourist attraction in the 20th century and was the source of many postcards during the 1940s and 1950s.

One postcard from 1952 depicted The Hermitage and boasted on the back:

> "It stands today just as it stood when he left it over 100 years ago, the classic home of Old Hickory. Although damaged by fire in 1834, it was restored immediately as it stands today."

Postcards also some times illustrate the General Andrew Jackson statue in Washington, D.C. Designed by Clark Mills, it is located in Lafayette Square. The bronze was cast from a cannon taken in Jackson's military campaigns.

President Andrew Jackson died at The Hermitage in 1845.

Presidential Site:
The Hermitage, Hermitage, Tennessee, 615-889-2941

Andrew Jackson. Engraved print; copyright 1901 The Gravure Company of America. $6-8

Andrew Jackson. Copyright 1902 by Colonial Press. $6-8

Andrew Jackson, seventh president. Real photo postcard. $4-5

President and Mrs. Jackson. Real photo postcard. $2-3

The Hermitage. Ca. 1960s postcard. $2-3

Tomb of General and Mrs. Andrew Jackson. Official Card of The Ladies Hermitage Association. $4-5

Jackson Statue, White House and Washington Monument, Washington, D. C.

Andrew Jackson. U.S. Presidents series, Topps Gum, 1956. $3-4

Jackson Statue, Washington, D.C. Early 1900s postcard. $3-4

Guest room at The Hermitage. Ca. 1960s postcard. $1-2

Parlors at The Hermitage. Ca. 1960s postcard. $1-2

Andrew Jackson

Martin Van Buren

President 1837 - 1841

Historians generally agree that Martin Van Buren was America's O.K. president. Not necessarily in his White House performance, but in being responsible for coining the actual word eternally meaning favorable or satisfactory.

During the presidential campaign of 1840 supporters of his candidacy formed the O.K. Club which was a kindly reference to Van Buren's home Old Kinderhook in New York State.

The campaign connection was forgotten over the decades but the catchy term O.K. took on a life and purpose of its own. By the 1880s it was even widely accepted in England. Early in the 20th century it had become the verbal version of the visionary thumbs-up worldwide.

Martin Van Buren, who would be the first native of the state of New York to be president, was born the son of a tavern keeper on December 5, 1782. By accident of birth Van Buren would be the first American president to be born as a United States citizen rather than under British rule.

The formative years of the man's life were relatively uneventful. Van Buren did not attend college nor did he serve in the military. He did become a lawyer and married Hannah Hoes in February of 1807.

While their marriage produced four children, it was ill-fated. Van Buren's wife died just 12 years after they were wedded leaving him the role of single parent. Despite the challenges Van Buren managed a progressive career in politics. Eventually he was elected U.S. Senator from New York, and in December of 1828 he left the job as senator to become governor of the state of New York.

As governor of the Empire State, and even before, Van Buren remain steadfast in his support of Andrew Jackson. During the presidential election of 1828 he was very effective in swinging votes to the Jackson camp. President Jackson acknowledged his efforts by appointing him Secretary of State early in his administration.

Van Buren survived a stormy term in the Jackson Cabinet and an appointment as Minister to the Court of St. James in good standing. In 1832 he became Jackson's running mate and was elected vice-president of the United States.

Ironically as big as Van Buren was in politics, in reality he was a relatively small man. Standing at five foot six inches, he was often described as a natty dresser, trim and dapper in appearance. He was known to like the late hours of the Washington life, and accordingly liked to sleep until noon even when vice presidential duties were pressing.

In 1836 Van Buren was nominated on the first ballot at the national convention of the Democrat-Republican Party. The Whig Party meanwhile nominated William Henry Harrison. The Whigs remained poorly organized however and ultimately their electoral support was divided among four candidates including Harrison and Daniel Webster.

The election was a double-win for the diminutive Van Buren. He carried 15 of the 26 existing states for a clear victory. At the same time among the four vice-president candidates none received a majority for the decision went to the U.S. Senate which selected Richard Johnson of Kentucky, Van Buren's original running mate.

When Van Buren took office in March of 1837 the widower took his four motherless sons with him. Both outgoing President Jackson and incoming President Van Buren welcomed crowds of unannounced visitors at the White House that day.

Unfortunately for Van Buren's term of office the nation fell under the grip of a crippling economy which lasted for many years. The Whigs ran Harrison again in 1840, better organized and eager for victory their sing-song slogan ended, "We'll beat Van, Van is a used-up man."

Van Buren's political luck dissolved at that point. He lost the national election in 1840. Four years after his defeat an attempt to secure his party's nomination for president failed. He ultimately lost on the ninth ballot to a relatively unknown contender named James Polk. In 1848 he ran for president for an unprecedented fourth time. This time he was on the ticket of the anti-slavery Free Soil Party. Although he garnered slightly more than ten percent of the popular vote, he got no electoral votes.

The former president remained a staunch opponent of slavery not only during his tenure in the White House but afterwards as well. As president he nixed the annexation of Texas largely because it appeared to add to the mix of states supporting slavery. At the time of his death Van Buren was said to be in full support of President Abraham Lincoln's freeing of the slaves.

America's eighth president died at his Lindenwald estate in Kinderhook on July 24, 1862. Noted author Washington Irving once spoke of him as "one of the gentlest men I have ever met."

Presidential Site:
Marin Van Buren National Historic Site, Kinderhook, New York, 518-758-9689

Martin Van Buren. Engraved print, copyright 1908, Bureau of National Literature and Art. $6-8

President and Mrs. Martin Van Buren. Real photo postcard. $2-3

Martin Van Buren, 8th president. Real photo postcard. $4-5

Martin Van Buren. Copyright 1902, The Colonial Press. $6-8

Van Buren as Vice President. Real photo postcard. $3-4

Martin Van Buren. Little Debbie premium card. $2-3

President Van Buren. Real photo postcard. $2-3

Lindenwald at Kinderhook. Posted 1907. $3-5

William Henry Harrison

President 1841

William Henry Harrison served in office for only one single month and yet achieved many firsts in White House history.

Harrison was the first president to die in office, and the first whose grandson would some day be president. He was the only president too whose First Lady never lived one single day in the official residence.

The person who would be the ninth president of the United States was born February 9, 1773 in Berkeley, Virginia. His father, Benjamin Harrison, had been a signer of the Declaration of Independence and a very active member of the Continental Congress.

William Henry, the last of the family's seven children, attended Hampden-Sydney College where he studied medicine. However instead of becoming a physician he accepted a commission in the military. Early on Harrison served as aid to General Anthony Wayne, and later won fame in the 1811 Battle of Tippecanoe against Indians of the Northwest Territory.

Once out of the military Harrison served as secretary to the governor of the Northwest Territory and later became governor of the Indiana Territory. As governor the 28-year-old Harrison made his home in Vincennes, Indiana. The majestic house where he lived at that time was known as Grouseland. In later years it was often referred to as the White House of the West.

The 12 years as governor of the Indiana Territory and the previous service at the Battle of Tippecanoe made Harrison nationally famous. It was no major surprise that his name came at the Whig Party's national convention.

Harrison was nominated on the second ballot of that convention. His running mate was John Tyler. Meanwhile, the Democratic-Republican Party nominated then sitting president Martin Van Buren by acclamation on the ballot or their convention.

By most all accounts the national presidential election of 1840 was a bang-up event rich with political slogans and enthusiastic rallies abounding. Supporters of Harrison offered slogans like "log cabin and hard cider" or "Tippecanoe and Tyler Too" making reference to the Indian battle and the last name of the vice-presidential candidate.

All the excitement proved to be a good year for the political process. According to Our Country's Presidents by Frank Freidel an amazing 78 percent of the eligible voters showed up at the polls. The number was double the amount of voters who took part in selecting a president just four years earlier.

In terms of raw numbers, the nationwide vote was close. Harrison defeated Van Buren by only 150,000 votes. In terms of the Electoral College however it was a flat knockout with Harrison carrying 26 states to his opponent's seven. The final Electoral College total ran to a very lopsided count of 234 to 60.

In January of 1841, Harrison boarded the steamer *S.S. Ben Franklin* going from Cincinnati to Washington, D.C.

Most of the family stayed at home including his wife, Anna Symmes Harrison. She planned to join her husband later but never did. Her First Lady duties at the White House were generally carried out by Harrison's daughter-in-law, Jane Irwin Harrison, who had traveled to Washington with the president.

That quirk in history made Harrison the only president whose spouse (not counting widowed or never married presidents) did not serve in the official residence. While George Washington did not live in the White House, his wife, Martha, lived and served in the official residence. John Adams eventually moved in the White House with his First Lady as second president.

At the time of his election Harrison was the oldest person to hold that high office.

On March 4, 1841 he rode a white horse from the White House to the Capitol before he delivered a withering 8,500 word inaugural speech. Hatless and coatless he spoke for one hour and 45 minutes in the cold and stormy weather. Next he rode horse in a two-hour parade before joining in three inaugural balls.

Most accounts say this recklessness resulted in a severe cold which in turn led to pneumonia. A few reports suggest that the serious illness did not arise until three weeks after the inauguration and may not have been the direct cause of his fatal illness.

At any rate he was bedridden by late March and died in the early morning of April 4, just a month after taking office.

Today he is buried at William Henry Harrison Memorial Park in North Bend, Ohio.

Just 48 years after his death, his grandson Benjamin Harrison became president of the United States. Thus they became the only grandfather and grandson combination to ever hold the American presidency.

Presidential Site:
William H. Harrison Mansion, Vincennes, Indiana, 812-882-2096

William Henry Harrison

Engravings of William H. Harrison from official portrait. Copyright 1901, The Gravure Company of America. $6-8

William Henry Harrison. Leighton Co. postcard. $8-10

President Wm. Harrison. Early 1900s postcard. $4-5

 Home of Harrison in Vincennes, Indiana. Early 20th century postcard. $2-3

Wm. Henry Harrison's Tomb. Ca. 1940s postcard. $2-3

Statue of William Harrison, Cincinnati, Ohio. Early 20th century postcard. $2-3

John Tyler

President John Tyler died unmourned and unacknowledged by United States government. In fact a Congressional act to memorialize his passing did not come until more than half a century later.

When he died in January of 1862 the Civil War was raging and Tyler did not consider himself a United States citizen. At the time he was preparing to serve a term in the House of Representatives of the Confederate Congress.

Tyler passed away under official allegiance to the Confederate States of America in Richmond, Virginia.

As a result, despite being a former American president, the federal government made no official announcement of Tyler's death in Washington, D.C. The nation's capitol remained totally silent on the matter.

The president, who for a time would become invisible to the federal government, was born on a working plantation in 1790 Virginia. He was one of eight children in a family living in Charles City County, Virginia.

An ambitious young man, Tyler graduated from college at age 17 and was a lawyer at age 19. By the time he was 21 he was serving in the Virginia House of Delegates, and the following year he married his first wife, Letitia Christian. By age 26 he was a member of the United States Congress.

At the age of 35 Tyler had become governor of Virginia, and would later become a United States Senator.

By the presidential election year of 1840 Tyler has switched from being a southern Democrat to become a vice presidential candidate on the Whig Party ticket. He became the running mate of William Henry Harrison, best known in the country for waging war with American Indians. As a team their campaign slogan became, "Tippecanoe and Tyler Too." The former representing one particular Indian battle and the later being the last name of the potential vice-president.

In March of 1841 Tyler was sworn-in to the office of vice president. He would serve in the office for just one month. President Harrison died on April 4 while his vice president was with his family in Williamsburg, Virginia. Two days later Tyler returned to Washington and took the oath of office for the presidency.

In doing so, Tyler recorded two White House firsts. Firstly, he became the first vice president to succeed to the presidency through death of a president. Secondly, that two-day period be-

tween Harrison's death and Tyler's oath was the longest in history for the nation to be without a president.

There was one more 'first' as Tyler continued into his presidential term. He became the first president to serve the entire term without a vice president. Additionally as he continued his term his relationship with the Whig Party was equally missing. Tyler fiercely opposed efforts and policies of the Whig Party to the point where he became the first president to face impeachment proceedings.

Adding further to the gloom of his term, Tyler's beloved wife, Letitia, died. Two years later he selected another young bride, Julia Gardiner, and they were married on his birthday in 1844. Julia, who was somehow nicknamed 'Rose of Long Island', served the nation as First Lady for eight months before the Tyler two left the White House for good.

Tyler remained involved in various political causes long after his presidency ended. Ultimately in 1861 the ex-president helped form and organize the Confederate States of America.

Politics and government aside, Tyler had an active family life as well. Between the two wives, he father 15 children—seven girls and eight boys—another presidential record. His last child, Pearly Tyler, was born when the former president was age 70.

Tyler's death in January of 1862 came just weeks before he was to assume office as a member of the newly established Congress of the Confederate States of America. While he was mourned in the capitol of the Confederacy, no mention of it was made in the capitol of the United States of America.

In 1911, more than 50 years after his death, the U.S. Congress authorized a monument be erected to honor his memory. In 1915 the monument was finally completed, and in October of that same year it was dedicated at Hollywood Cemetery in Richmond. The dedication ceremony itself was attended by five U.S. congressmen and five U.S. senators.

Presidential Site:
Berkeley Plantation, Charles City, Virginia,
    804-829-6018
Sherwood Forest, Charles City County, Virginia,
    804-829-5377

John Tyler

President John Tyler. Engraved print. Copyright 1901, The Gravure Company of America. $6-8

John Tyler. Real photo postcard. $2-3

Julia Tyler. Real photo postcard. $2-3

Tyler as Vice President. Real photo postcard. $3-4

President Tyler and Second Wife. Real photo postcard. $2-3

John Tyler, 10th President. Leighton Co. postcard. $6-8

John Tyler

TENTH PRESIDENT   1841-1845

BORN-1790   DIED-1862

P-10 BECK

Tenth President. Real photo postcard. $5-6

10

John Tyler
1841-1845
Born: March 29, 1790
Died: January 18, 1862
Party: Whig
Home State: VA
Occupation: Lawyer
VP: None
Notable Event: Trade Treaty with China
Fun Fact: President with the most children (16)

Little Debbie
Snack Cakes

John Tyler 1841-1845. Little Debbie premium card. $2-3

Letitia Tyler. Real photo postcard. $2-3

President John Tyler and first wife.

President Tyler and First Wife. Real photo postcard. $3-4

James Polk

President 1845 - 1849

Most historians will attest that America's 11th president, James Knox Polk, was the first and perhaps the ultimate 'dark horse' candidate for the White House.

Polk had absolutely no chance for the job in 1844. He was on no one's list and not even being mentioned as a contender.

Initially the battle that memorable year for the Democrat presidential nomination appeared to be clearly between former President Martin Van Buren and Lewis Cass, a military hero and former Secretary of War under President Andrew Jackson.

During the first seven ballots at the national convention in Baltimore there was no mention of Polk. Finally, on the eighth ballot with the support of former President Andrew Jackson, Polk was mentioned as a compromise candidate between Cass and Van Buren; it worked. On the ninth ballot, after all the tumult and shouting, Polk won the nomination on a unanimous vote.

Polk's running mate that year was George Dallas of Pennsylvania. The two faced powerful Whig Party presidential candidate Henry Clay and his vice president nominee Theodore Frelinghuysen. However Clay, like Van Buren had earlier, strongly opposed the annexation of Texas and extending the country further west to the Pacific Ocean. Polk favored it.

Ultimately the nation went with the expansionist views of Polk. He won more than 60 percent of the electorate vote.

The would-be president was born in 1795 in Meckenburg County, North Carolina.

In 1816 Polk's father Samuel Polk used handmade bricks to build the family's new home in Columbia, Tennessee. Decades later President Polk would become the first native of North Carolina to be elected president, and only the third to be elected president from a state other than his birth state.

Polk became a lawyer by occupation and in 1824 he married Sarah Childress. The following year they moved to his boyhood home on West Seventh Street in Columbia and lived there for many years.

After being elected to Congress, Polk rose to become Speaker of the U.S. House of Representatives. Later he was elected governor of the state of Tennessee.

The next leap up the political ladder was his remarkable 'dark horse' nomination and subsequent election as president of the United States.

Polk took office in 1845, the same year not surprisingly that the state of Texas was admitted to the Union. Trouble erupted the following year at the Mexican border. President Polk sent troops under the command of General Zachary Taylor to deal with the situation, when the federal force was reportedly attacked, Polk declared war against Mexico. The war basically ended with the U.S. annexing not only California but much additional southwestern territory.

Throughout his White House years President Polk was known for his hearty work ethic. Accounts say he rose at dawn and often labored at his desk until well after midnight. Before calling it a night, Polk then carefully recorded the details of his long day in his personal diary.

In 1848 a busy President Polk laid the cornerstone for the grand George Washington monument. That same year Wisconsin was admitted as the 30th state in a rapidly growing Union.

Polk declined to seek re-election, due to part to his declining health. Some historians conclude that the tireless efforts and long hours in the White House took its toll on him. He left Washington in 1849 to return to the less stressful life of retirement in Tennessee.

The former president chose his life with Mrs. Polk, to what had become known as Polk Place, in Nashville, Tennessee. Polk died in that home only three months after leaving life in the White House.

In June of 1849 one newspaper account grimly noted, "It is probably that the arduous duties of the Presidency had snapped the constitution of Mr. Polk."

Upon his death, friend and historian George Bancroft praised Polk as "one of the very best and most honest and most successful presidents this country ever had."

Despite Polk's implicit wishes that Polk Place ultimately to become the property of the state of Tennessee, that did not happen. After Mrs. Polk's death, the historic site was demolished in 1901.

President Polk and his wife Sarah are buried together on the grounds of the State Capitol in Nashville, Tennessee.

Presidential Sites:

James K. Polk Memorial Association, Columbia, Tennessee, 931-388-2354

Pres. James K. Polk State Historic Site, Pineville, North Carolina, 704-889-7145

James K. Polk. Real photo postcard. $4-5

James K. Polk. Colonial Bread premium card. 1976.
$2-3

Mrs. Polk and President Polk. Postcard from portraits of the couple.
$3-4

James Knox Polk. Real photo postcard. $2-3

President and Mrs. James Polk. Real photo postcard. $3-4

Postcard from portraits of President and Mrs. Polk. James Knox Polk Ancestral Home. Ca. 1950s. $3-4

Home of President James Polk. Woldridge Drug Co. postcard. Posted 1937. $2-3

Bronze bust of President Polk. Polk Home postcard. $2-3

Tomb of President Polk. Capitol Grounds postcard. $2-3

Parlor and Dining Room of Polk Home. Ca. 1950s postcard. $2-3

Zachary Taylor

President 1849 - 1850

While others including George Washington had experience in the military, Zachary Taylor was the first fully professional soldier to become president of the United States.

Most accounts say the war-hero tobacco chewing general was so non-political that he had never even voted in an election during his military career. Others say he voted once at age 62 just two years before being elected to office.

Others would follow the path from professional soldier to the White House including U.S. Grant and Dwight Eisenhower, but Taylor became the first in 1848.

The man who would become the 12th president of the U.S. was born in 1784 in Montebello, Virginia. Taylor became a soldier early in his life and remained in the military for decades.

Taylor married Margaret Mackall Smith in 1810 near Louisville, Kentucky. Two years later he was serving as an officer in the War of 1812. Later he would emerge as a distinguished military leader during the Mexican War of 1846.

At the Whig Party national convention just two years later the popular general was an early contender. Taylor was nominated on the fourth ballot, and his running mate was Millard Fillmore. The two defeated Democratic Party contenders were Lewis Cass and William Butler. Both candidates carried an equal number of the 30 states then in the Union, however Taylor won with more than 56 percent of the electoral votes.

"I never had an aspiration for the Presidency, nor have I now," commented the reluctant General the year of his election. "Nor would I have it on any other terms than I stated which the subject was first agitated…that my acceptance must be without pledges, so I could be the President of the whole nation and not of a Party."

Ironically Zachary Taylor was one of only two presidents who were members of the Whig Party.

As Taylor had declared, his greater concern was about unity of the country at the time of great division over slavery. Although he had owned a number of slaves at one time, Taylor generally favored a preserved Union "at all hazards."

Taylor's relatively brief tenure in the highest office in the land was not all that glamorous. His military horse Old Whitey was given free reign, so to speak, of the White House lawn. His wife Margaret arrived at the White House in poor health and largely avoided any First Lady activities.

On a hot Fourth of July afternoon in 1850 President Taylor attended the cornerstone laying ceremonies for the Washington Monument. Vari-ous reports indicate he consumed a large amount of food including cold cherries, ice milk, pickled cucumbers, and wild berries. By evening Taylor had become ill, and five days later he died. Today historians still disagree on President Taylor's precise cause of death with opinions ranging from gastroenteritis to cholera morbus.

Despite some written accounts, Taylor was not the first president to die in office. The first president to die in office was William Henry Harrison who died in April of 1841 of pneumonia just a month after taking office. Taylor was the second president to die in office.

Again there is controversy regarding the last rites given President Taylor. One version has it that he was quietly buried in the family crypt five days after his death with little ceremony. Other accounts however indicate his death was given much more attention in Washington.

A Washington newspaper carried this account:

"He breathed his last at thirty-five minutes past 10 o'clock, yesterday evening, and lies in State this morning at the Executive mansion, surrounded by his grief stricken and afflicted family."

Today the soldier who became president is buried in the Zachary Taylor National Cemetery near Louisville, Kentucky.

Zachary Taylor. Engraved print, copyright 1908 by Bureau of National Literature and Art. $8-10

Zachary Taylor

Left:
Zachary Taylor Monument in Louisville, Kentucky. Posted 1909. $2-3

Middle:
Zachary Taylor. Early 1900s postcard. $6-8

Right:
Zachary Taylor. Real photo postcard. $4-5

Residence of Bettie Dandridge, President Taylor's daughter. Posted 1912. $2-3

President and Mrs. Taylor. Real photo postcard. $3-4

Springfield, Home of President Taylor. Caufield & Shook postcard. $3-4

Birthplace of Zachary Taylor. Real photo postcard. $2-3

Millard Fillmore

President 1850 - 1853

The person who finally brought books to the White House was First Lady Abigail Fillmore, a former schoolteacher with a fiery interest in education.

When President Millard Fillmore and Mrs. Fillmore first arrived at the White House the place was bookless, lacking even a Bible. Lady Abigail commandeered a large room on the second floor of the White House and made it a library. The first books on the shelves were actually from the Fillmore family's collection.

Abigail's love of books had actually led to romance between her and the future president.

Millard Fillmore had only a meager formal education in a one-room school not far from his home in Cayuga County, New York. While attending there he fell in love with his comely red-hair school teacher Abigail Powers. Many years later they married and Abigail continued to tutor Millard the rest of their married life.

The 15th president of the United States was born January 7, 1800. Like Abe Lincoln, Fillmore too was born in a log cabin. Unlike Lincoln however the Fillmore cabin was not preserved and only a replica of it exists at a state park in New York State.

He was the second child in what would become a family of nine. The family was of little means, and consequently Fillmore was sent off to learn the clothing trade at age 15. Shockingly he would become the nation's first and only president with a legitimate background as an indentured servant.

In later years Fillmore managed to study law with the help of an acting judge in Cayuga County. He eventually passed the bar exam, married his school days sweetheart, and established a law office in Buffalo, New York.

Soon Fillmore developed an interest in politics, and in 1833 he was elected to the U.S. House of Representatives. While he was re-elected to the post in Congress, his bid for governor of New York in 1844 as a Whig Party candidate failed.

Fillmore's political fortunes had improved considerably by 1848 when he won the Whig nomination for vice president. Months later he was elected in the national election. The following March he took office along with President Zachary Taylor.

When Taylor died in 1850, Fillmore assumed the presidency. At the time, in the middle of the 19th century, he was only the second vice president in history to succeed a president who had died in office.

First Lady Abigail immediately set about providing the White House with its first library. Besides their own personal supply of books, the President and Mrs. Fillmore persuaded Congress to assist. In March of 1851 an act of Congress put aside $250 for the purchase of books for the Executive Mansion during the direction of the president.

On the whole Fillmore's term in the White House however was brief and bitter. California was admitted to the Union and the Washington Territory was created out of the northern part of Oregon. However the bigger picture was the sharp division over slavery. Fillmore brokered the Great Compromise of 1850 which managed to displease those on both sides of the issue.

By 1852, after having served well less than three years on the job, the Whig Party had had its fill of Fillmore as did most of the rest of the country. At their national convention the Whigs bypassed Fillmore giving the nomination to General Winfield Scott instead. However their choice was unsuccessful and the cause was equally unsuccessful. Ironically Fillmore would be the country's last Whig president.

Millard's beloved wife Abigail, who also installed the White House's first bath tub, became ill while attending the inauguration of President Franklin Pierce. She died a short time later. Abigail was 55.

Undaunted by two staggering losses former President Fillmore accepted the presidential nomination of the American Party in 1856. Nicknamed the Know-Nothing Party for its organized claim to 'know nothing' about politics, the party and their candidate lost decisively in the election that year to James Buchanan.

Fillmore more or less retired in the years that followed to his elaborate home on 52 Niagara Street in Buffalo. As he grew older the former president spoke out against President Abraham Lincoln. However he fully supported President Andrew Johnson during the post Civil War Reconstruction period.

An article in the prestigious Saturday Evening Post suggested that Fillmore spent his twilight years in odd activities including reading Shakespeare to shoe factory workers near his home.

Presidential Site:
Millard Fillmore House Museum, East Aurora, New York, 716-652-8875

Millard Fillmore. Engraved print.
Copyright 1908 by Bureau of National
Literature and Art. $5-6

President and Mrs. Fillmore. Real photo postcard. $3-4

As Vice
President. Real
photo postcard.
$2-3

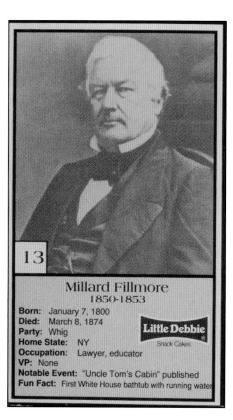

President Millard Fillmore. Little Debbie
premium card. 1992. $2-3

U.S. Presidents Series.
Topps gum card.
1972. $2-3

Thirteenth President. Real photo
postcard. $5-6

President Fillmore. Illinois Postcard Co.
postcard. Early 1900s. $5-6

The 13th President. Leighton Co. postcard.
$6-8

Millard Fillmore Residence. Early 1900s postcard. $4-5

Franklin Pierce

President 1853 - 1857

Franklin Pierce, America's 14th president, was the only president who did not swear. This unusual trait however applied not to profanity but to taking the oath of office.

Presidents before and after Pierce elected to take the oath of office by simply saying, "I do solemnly swear" to the duties of the office and to the Constitution.

Pierce felt differently.

Article 2 of section one of the U.S. Constitution stipulates that the President may actually substitute "I do solemnly affirm" rather than "swear". Pierce chose to 'affirm.'

Afterwards, on his inaugural, he stepped to the lectern and delivered more than 3,000 words without reference to notes, text, or teleprompter. Until Pierce came along, other presidents had just read their comments rather actually delivering a speech.

Born in 1804, Pierce would become the first president of the 19th century. He was the sixth of eight children living in Hillsborough, New Hampshire. Later he attended college with the likes of Nathaniel Hawthorne and Henry Wadsworth Longfellow, when he studied law.

An ambitious young Pierce served in the New Hampshire legislature when he was only 24. Next he became a member of Congress, and by age 32 had become a United States Senator. Eventually he resigned the position of senator because his wife Jane Appleton Pierce disliked life in Washington, and he thought he could make a better income in his law firm back in New Hampshire.

As far as the presidency itself, Pierce once declared the office "would be utterly repugnant to my tastes and wishes." Apparently he changed his mind.

During the presidential election year of 1852 Franklin Pierce was not in serious consideration. When the Democrat Party held its convention the delegates cast 47 ballots without mentioning his name. Pierce began to get some votes on the 48th ballot and but the 49th ballot he had the nomination.

Historians say the party went with Pierce because of his distinguished military record and his political balance. He was considered a friend of the South, but still somewhat of a moderate living in the North.

In the general election Pierce's opposition was the Whig Party's General Winfield Scott. General Scott had won a national reputation as a military leader during the Mexican War. The Whig Party however was in disarray internally while the public had grown impatient with their party's President Millard Fillmore.

While Pierce generally refused to campaign and made no political speeches, he never the less carried 27 of the existing 31 states.

Tragically Franklin and Jane's 11-year-old son was killed in a railway crash as the family was making its way from New Hampshire to Washington, D.C. A grief-stricken Mrs. Pierce returned home and did not attend her husband's inauguration.

Aside from the lengthy speech by President Pierce, the inauguration event itself was a modest one. The inaugural ball was canceled because the family was still in mourning. The overall cost of the event was modest as well. The cost of erecting the platform and later disassembling it, plus the pay for 16 extra policemen totaled $322.

Jane Pierce finally did come to Washington, but she remained in mourning. Accounts say the woman, who had lost two other children earlier, always wore black while in the White House. A relative, Abby Kent Means, generally acted as White House hostess during the Pierce term.

As for Pierce the country and even the Cabinet remained highly divided during his presidency. Pierce never made a single change in his Cabinet, even keeping on Secretary of War Jefferson Davis. Davis later would become president of the Confederacy during the Civil War.

To his disappointment the Democrat Party declined to nominate President Pierce for a second term in 1856, so he returned home to New Hampshire. Even there he remained relatively obscure.

Pierce died on October 8, 1869. He was buried at Concord's North Cemetery beside his wife and three children. In 1914 the state of New Hampshire erected a bronze statue of Pierce on the corner of its capitol grounds. In 1946 a granite memorial was finally placed at his gravesite.

Presidential Site:
Franklin Pierce Homestead, Hillsborough, New Hampshire, 603-478-3913

President Franklin Pierce. Engraved print, copyright 1908 by Bureau of National Literature and Art. $6-8

Page from the book *Abraham Lincoln* by Charles Coffin, 1893, features drawing of Franklin Pierce.

CONFLICT BETWEEN FREEDOM AND SLAVERY.   141

who should enjoy their civil and ...g to slavery a region of country larger than ...es of the Union.

...nimated Douglas to violate his pledges never ...ny people thought him to have been sincere in ...eved he was influenced by an ardent desire to ...pted to secure the prize by doing what the ...e. He saw nothing immoral or wrong in hold- ...men in the Northern States did not regard ...sinful. It might or it might not be beneficial ...people of a Territory wanted slavery as one of ...s was willing they should have it.

...he morality of the act which violated a solemn ...re the extension of slavery, Douglas, Davis, and ...nsider that for national wrong-doing there had ...e eternal law : an eye for an eye, a tooth for a ...to them that divine Providence might have ...arrying out the plan. The booming of the ...was heard in every city and town throughout ...was seen that the first movement of the slave- ...possession of Kansas, and there was therefore ...e that Territory to freedom. The Free State ...tablishing of towns, schools, colleges, churches, ...n and women, who should enjoy their civil and ...onstitution guar- ...lave Party deter- ...utiful region to ...y. The struggle began, the slave-holders of Missouri taking possession of the lands nearest the terri- torial line in advance of any settlers from the Free States. A society was formed in Massachusetts to aid emigrants. It was a national society, and Abraham Lincoln was one of the Executive Committee ; but there is no evidence that he was actively engaged in promoting the settlement of the Territory. The first party of settlers from Massachusetts reached Kansas, and laid out the town of Lawrence, naming it in honor of Mr. Amos A. Lawrence, the president of the society. The poet Whittier wrote a

FRANKLIN PIERCE.

FRANKLIN PIERCE.

Franklin Pierce
1853-1857

President Franklin Pierce. Illinois Postcard Co. postcard. 1902. $5-6

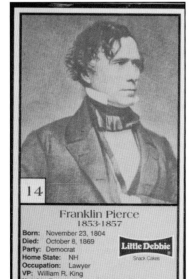

14

Franklin Pierce
1853-1857

Born: November 23, 1804
Died: October 8, 1869
Party: Democrat
Home State: NH
Occupation: Lawyer
VP: William R. King
Notable Event: Kansas-Nebraska Act
Fun Fact: First to do his inaugural speech from memory

Little Debbie Snack Cakes

Franklin Pierce. Little Debbie premium card. 1993. $2-3

Room of Ex. President Franklin Pierce, House, Hillsboro, N. H.

Interior of Franklin Pierce House. Early 1900s postcard. $3-4

James Buchanan

President 1857 - 1861

James Buchanan was America's first and only life-long bachelor president.

In later years President Grover Cleveland entered the White House as a single person, but he eventually wed while still president. The ceremony with Frances Folsom became one of the biggest social events of his administration.

Buchanan never made it to wedded bliss—before, during, or even after his White House days.

"Old Buck," as he was sometimes fondly called, did encounter early romance.

Historians suggest Buchanan as a young and highly successful lawyer courted Anne Carline Coleman. They met in the summer of 1819 and were soon engaged to be married. Trouble came however amid rumors of Buchanan's casual misdeeds. An unhappy Anne even penned a 'Dear John' letter to the future president abruptly ending the relationship. Buchanan is said to have denied any wrongdoing, and vainly attempted to reunite the two.

In December of that same year Miss Coleman ended her life with an overdose of laudanum, otherwise known as tincture of opium. It was never determined whether the deadly dosage was accidental or deliberate.

The future president was born in a log cabin on April 23, 1791 in Cove Gap, Pennsylvania. He was the second child in what would be a family of 11.

As humble as his beginnings were, Buchanan rose to become a noted attorney who reportedly had already amassed $300,000 before he was 21 years of age. Still ambitious he went on to serve as a member of Congress and later as a United States Senator.

An eager Buchanan made three futile attempts to win the Democrat Party's nomination for President. After unsuccessful trying in 1844 and again in 1848, was still denied the nomination in 1852. Finally in 1856, on a tedious 17th ballot, Buchanan was nominated as the party's choice to lead the national ticket.

That year the campaign motto called for the election of Buck and Breck. Buck being Buchanan's nickname and Beck standing for his running mate, John Breckenridge. In the political lexicon of that era, Buchanan was known as a 'doughface' or one who was a northern politician supporting the so-called cause of the South.

In the presidential election that year Buchanan faced Republican contender James C. Fremont. The newly formed Republican Party was largely an accord of antislavery segments of the Whig Party and the Freed Democrat Party. That year Buchanan rolled up a victory of about 500,000 votes. He garnered nearly 60 percent of the electoral vote.

Buchanan was inaugurated on March 4, 1857. Still very much the bachelor, he was the nation's 15th president.

Following the inaugural there was a lavish parade featuring giant floats and large crowds of curious people lining the long parade route. In anticipation of such an event a special building had been constructed on Judiciary Square. There were 6,000 guests for the gala inaugural ball.

The White House itself was not that lavish or so gala. The structure was lit by gas. Before departing President Franklin Pierce had installed a furnace, but meals were cooked on a large iron stove provided even earlier by President Millard Fillmore. The newly arrived Buchanan moved to replace the French made furnishings with furniture made in America.

Reportedly Buchanan did not live in the dreary White House during the summer months due in part to the threat of malaria in the mosquito-infested swamps nearby. There were rumors that the place should become merely an office for the president, and not a residence.

On the bright side at the White House, there was the official Mistress of the place, Buchanan's niece, Harriet Lance. A statuesque beauty of 25, the lovely Harriet was the daughter of Buchanan's sister. Harriet's mother had died when the girl was seven years old, and her father died shortly afterwards. Ultimately Harriet came to live with her uncle James, and eventually she became the official hostess of the White House.

The presidential niece reportedly did a splendid job of carrying out the social chores of the White House. Some accounts say she as the inspiration for the popular song, Listen For The Mocking Bird, written by Septimus Winner.

In 1858 Buchanan became the first president to exchange transatlantic telegrams while in office. Greetings in this case involved trading words with Queen Victoria in England.

If the Buchanan years as president were lackluster, so were the president's own feelings about it.

"I am now in my sixty-ninth year and am heartily tired of my position as president," Buchanan wrote Mrs. James Knox Polk as his term wound down in late 1859. "I shall leave it in the beginning of March 1861, should a kind Providence prolong my days, until that period, with much greater satisfaction than when entering on the duties of the office."

As President Abraham Lincoln took office, Buchanan retired to his beloved Wheatland near Lancaster, Pennsylvania. He had purchased the splendid estate back in 1848 for total of $6,750.

President Buchanan died in June of 1868 and is buried at Woodward Hill Cemetery near there.

Presidential Site:
James Buchanan Foundation, Lancaster, Pennsylvania, 717-392-8721

President Buchanan. Leighton Co. postcard. $6-8

Home at Wheatland. Print of original drawing. $5-6

James Buchanan. Colonial Bread premium card. 1976. $2-3

James Buchanan. Engraved print from official portrait. $5-6

The 15th President. Mirro-Krome postcard. $3-5

Wheatland, Home of President Buchanan. Posted 1932. $2-3

Abraham Lincoln

President 1861 - 1865

Abraham Lincoln, possibility the most re-membered and revered of our American Presidents, owned only one house in his entire life.

The only place President Lincoln truly called home was a modest house in Springfield, Illinois.

Lincoln purchased the home in May of 1844 and lived there with his family until he was elected president of the United States. In all he spent 17 years living there in the tan colored "Quaker brown" residence.

The first American president to be assassinated, President Lincoln never returned to the house in Springfield.

On February 11, 1861 Lincoln departed from Springfield and his home for the White House. Upon leaving he told well-wishers, "I now leave, not knowing when or whether I may return, with a task before me greater than that which rested on Washington."

Lincoln was born in February 12, 1809 to Thomas and Nancy Hanks Lincoln at Hodgenville, Kentucky. The birth of the person who would be the 16th president of the U.S. took place in the humblest of primitive log cabins. It had one room and a dirt floor.

Two years later Thomas Lincoln moved his family to another squabble of land with an equally shabby cabin near Knob Creek. In 1816 the family moved to the Indiana wilderness. Two years later Nancy Lincoln died of 'milk sickness' and was buried near there. The Lincoln family struggled for another year before Thomas took a second wife. The woman, a widow, brought three of own children to the modest Lincoln cabin.

Young Abe Lincoln grew up with little formal education. He often studied at home and did general farm work. When he was 22 he clerked in a store at New Salem, Illinois. Later he later joined military volunteers fighting the Black Hawk War, and eventually became postmaster there at New Salem.

For eight years Lincoln served as a member of the Illinois State Legislature, and during that time he also studied law. The next advancement for Lincoln was his election on the Whig Party ticket to the U.S. House of Representatives. He served one two-year term before establishing a law practice in Springfield, Illinois.

An ambitious Lincoln became the Republican candidate for U.S. Senator in 1858 and consequently attracted national attention through a series of popular debates with his Democratic opponent Senator Stephen Douglas. Lincoln lost the election but won much public acclaim.

Just two years later, in 1860, Lincoln was nominated as the Republican Party's presidential candidate on the third ballot. He would ultimately face two other major candidates, National Democrat Party nominee John Breckinridge and Constitutional Union Party nominee John Bell.

It was during that presidential election that Lincoln began growing a beard. It was largely at the behest of an 11-year-old girl living in Springfield. She suggested he grow "whiskers" to attract more of the voters in her family. He did grow them, and personally visited the little girl to thank her.

After a vigorous campaign Lincoln managed to win the election and 59 percent of the Electoral College vote. The country however remained bitterly divided.

At the presidential inauguration there appeared a bearded Lincoln, standing six foot four inches, weighing about 180 pounds, dark complexioned, with grey eyes and coarse black hair. Shortly before noon he was driven down Pennsylvania Avenue in the open carriage of President James Buchanan. The carriage carrying Lincoln drove immediately by the as yet unfinished dome of the Capitol building.

On the east portico of the Capitol building outgoing President Buchanan greeting him by saying, "If you are as happy, my dear sir, on entering this house as I am on leaving it and returning home, you are the happiest man on earth."

Barely a month after Lincoln took the oath of office; the Civil War erupted and continued for four brutal and bloody years. In the midst of it all Lincoln signed the Emancipation Proclamation which freed the slaves in Confederate territory. An original painting of Lincoln reviewing that document with members of the Cabinet once hung in the Capitol building.

Despite the torment of it all President Lincoln found time on occasion to spend with his young son Thomas. The lad was nicknamed Tad because his father felt the boy looked like a tadpole in that his head was too large for his body. To the White House staff however the youngster was bothersome and at times was called the Little Tyrant for his bratty behavior.

During the presidential election of 1864 Lincoln received 90 percent of the existing electoral vote. His Democrat Party opponent George McClellan won just nine percent of the electoral vote. The eleven Confederate States did not vote that year.

On April 14, 1865 just a few days after the surrender of Confederate General Robert E. Lee

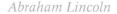

at Appomattox Court House, President Lincoln was assassinated. He was shot in the head by actor John Wilkes Booth using a.44 caliber derringer at Ford's Theater.

Lincoln died the following day. He was, oddly enough, the first president to have been born in a state that was not one of the original 13 Colonies.

America mourned the passing of the President with great emotion and in great numbers. He was, after all, the first president to be assassinated. Millions are said to have lined the railroad tracks as the body of Lincoln was carried from Washington to his home in Springfield. He was later also honored by the Lincoln Memorial in Washington, D.C.

President Lincoln was buried at Oak Ridge Cemetery in Springfield. He was 56.

Presidential Sites:

Ford's Theater National Historic Site, Washington, District of Columbia, 202-426-6830

Lincoln Home National Historic Site, Springfield, Illinois, 217-492-4241

Illinois State Historical Library, Springfield, Illinois, 217-492-4241

Lincoln Boyhood National Memorial, Lincoln, Indiana 812-937-4541

Abraham Lincoln Birthplace National Historic Site

The Lincoln Museum, Fort Wayne, Indiana, 219-455-3864

Abraham Lincoln Presidential Library, Springfield, Illinois, 217-492-4241

A. Lincoln. Engraved print; copyright 1908 by Bureau of National Literature and Art. $8-10

The Proclamation of Emancipation

Proclamation of Emancipation. Print, copyright 1908 by Bureau of National Literature and Art. $8-10

Abraham Lincoln

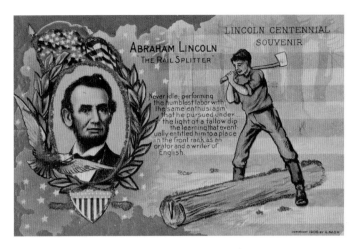

Lincoln Centennial postcard. Early 1900s. $8-10

Lincoln and Gen. Grant Print. $8-10

President Lincoln. Postcard based on Matthew Brady portrait. Parks & History Association. $2-3

President Lincoln in Richmond. Print. $8-10

Lincoln Cabin. Lincoln Log Cabin State Park postcard. $2-3

Lincoln birthplace. Nancy Lincoln Inn postcard, Hodgenville, Kentucky. $2-3

President Lincoln. Scenic South Card Co. postcard. $2-3

Cooper Shop. New Salem State Park postcard New Salem, Illinois. $2-3

Family Cabin, ca. 1816. Postcard image of Thomas Lincoln Family Cabin. Lincoln Boyhood National Memorial at Lincoln City, Indiana. $2-3

Abraham Lincoln

Lincoln home in Springfield, Illinois. State Memorial postcard. $2-3

Abraham Lincoln. Curteichrom postcard. $3-5

Rutledge Tavern. New Salem State Park postcard in New Salem, Illinois. $2-3

Gettysburg Address. L.E. Smith postcard. $3-4

Lincoln's Speech Memorial in Gettysburg, Pa.. L.E. Smith postcard. $1-2

Lincoln Memorial, Washington, D.C. B.S. Reynolds Co. postcard. $1-2

Grave of Nancy Hanks. Nancy Hanks Lincoln Park postcard. $3-4

Nancy Hanks Lincoln Hall. Photograph Lincoln City, Indiana. $2-3

Lincoln-Douglas Debate marker. L.L. Cook Co. postcard. Copyright 1960. $2-3

Burial plot of Lincoln's parents. Shiloh Cemetery postcard near Mattoon, Illinois. $2-3

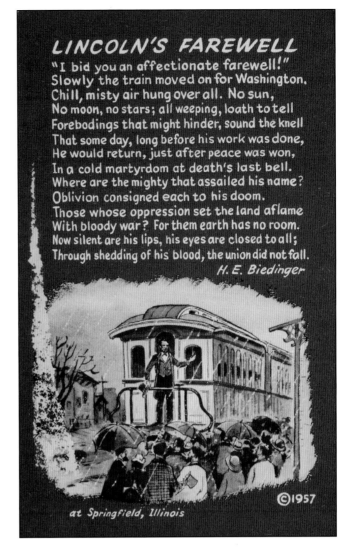

Lincoln's Farewell. Postcard promoting the book *Sonnets & Short Poems About Lincoln and Other Great Men*. Copyright 1957. $3-4

The Martyred President. Early 1900s postcard. $8-10

Abraham Lincoln

President Lincoln. Lincoln National Historical Park
postcard Hodgenville, Kentucky. $5-6

Lincoln Monument, Lincoln Park, Chicago.
Early 1900s postcard. $4-5

Lincoln National Memorial, Kentucky. Lincoln
National Historical Park postcard. $2-3

Lincoln Statue, Fort Wayne, Indiana. Ca. 1940s postcard. $2-3

Lincoln Statue,
Washington, D.C.
Posted 1908. $4-5

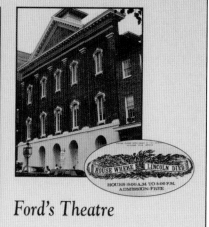

Ford's
Theatre.
Capsco Inc.
postcard.
$1-2

Andrew Johnson

President 1865 - 1869

Historians now note that Andrew Johnson was America's first, and thus far only, home-schooled president.

Johnson, who came to the White House upon the assassination of President Abraham Lincoln, never ever sat in a schoolroom. Instead he was taught to read and write by his teenaged bride. She managed to make him a pretty good public speaker too.

The person who would be the 17th American president was born in poverty December 29, 1808 in Raleigh, North Caroline. He was the third of three children and the family literally lived in a shack.

Johnson's father died when Andrew was very young and the family struggled just to survive. Eventually Johnson and his brother were 'bound out' as indentured servants to a tailor. The practice, common in the 19th century, usually involved a commitment on the part of the 'indentured' to work without wages for a long length of time. It could be what was required to pay a family debt, or in some cases donated labor to learn a trade.

At any rate most accounts indicate Johnson eventually fled that situation and ended up practicing the tailoring trade in Greenville, Tennessee. It was there that he met and married Eliza McCardle. She was 16, and he was 18 going on 19. According to White House records that wedding made Johnson the American president who married at the youngest age.

Much more importantly to Johnson was the fact that Eliza became his full time school teacher. Some stories say she read to him every night while he labored at tailoring. She apparently schooled him fairly well at public speaking too, and he began to join in public debates of various issues.

The 'home-schooled' Johnson did well enough to become elected mayor of that small town as well maintain a successful business. He later served in the Tennessee legislature and the U.S. House of Representatives. At age 49 he became a United States Senator.

At the onset of the Civil War only Johnson remained in Washington when all other senators representing the Southern states withdrew and joined the Confederacy. Johnson however stayed and staunchly supported maintaining the Union. Grateful for his support President Lincoln appointed Johnson as military governor of Tennessee for a brief period.

In 1864 the National Union Party selected 'War Democrat' Johnson as Lincoln's running mate. It was a surprise move to many political observers of the day, however it indeed put a Southerner on the ticket. What ever the strategy it elected the Lincoln-Johnson team.

Much has been written about Johnson's condition at the 1865 inaugural. Accounts say Johnson was very much under the influence of alcohol during the ceremony. Some reports blame a long carriage ride and a previous illness for his conditions. Other sources hint at a continuing drinking problem.

Tragedy stuck the following spring. Lincoln died from an assassin's bullet early in the morning of April 15, 1865. At 10 a.m. that Saturday morning Johnson was given the oath of office at the very informal Kirkwood House in Washington. Less than a year after being a 'surprise' selection on the ticket Johnson had become the President of the United States.

Johnson came to the White House in a difficult position. The soon to be re-admitted South hated him, and the North strongly suspected his intentions. Moreover his dedicated teacher and wife, Eliza, was ill with tuberculosis. The duties of First Lady were therefore generally carried out by their daughter Martha Johnson Patterson.

President Johnson moved to provide amnesty and bring the Confederate states back into the Union. However many objected to his methods and when he dismissed Secretary of War Edwin Stanton, the House of Representatives voted to impeach him. The impeachment trial in the Senate lasted for two months. Ultimately the vote was one short of the required two-thirds majority and the effort to oust Johnson failed. He had been the first American president in history to be impeached.

Johnson sought the presidential nomination in 1868 but was rejected.

After leaving the White House for good and returning home, Johnson was still drawn to politics. He eventually was again elected a U.S. Senator from Tennessee.

In 1875 the former president suffered a stroke while at his home in Greenville and died four months later. He is buried at Andrew Johnson National Cemetery in Greenville.

Presidential Site:
Andrew Johnson National Historic Site, Greenville, Tennessee, 615-638-3551

Andrew Johnson

Andrew Johnson. Little Debbie premium
card. 1992. $1-2

Birthplace of Andrew Johnson. James Thiem postcard. $3-5

Andrew Johnson. Engraved print. Copyright 1908
by Bureau of National Literature And Art. $6-8

Andrew Johnson. Colonial Bread premium card. 1976. $2-3

Home of Andrew Johnson. Andrew National Monument postcard. $2-3

Andrew Johnson house in Greenville, Tennessee. Johnson National Historic Site postcard. $2-3

Andrew Johnson homestead parlor. Johnson National Historic Site postcard. $2-3

Andrew Johnson bedroom. Johnson National Historic Site postcard. $2-3

Andrew Johnson Tailor Shop. Johnson National Historic Site postcard. $2-3

Ulysses S. Grant

President 1869 - 1877

The question about who was buried in Grant's Tomb was a regular feature of the Groucho Marx radio and TV shows of the 1950s.

It was not a trick question. Rather it was a question with an obvious answer intended to reward quiz show contestants who had otherwise won nothing.

President U.S. Grant's own grandson, a university professor, actually even appeared on Groucho's popular You Bet Your Life program in 1953.

Possibly a more challenging question today would be who appears on the $50 dollar bill, and has been featured on many postcards? The answer again would be President Grant.

In terms of postcards there are many of Grant's Tomb which was a very popular tourist attraction early in the 20th century. Lots of other Grant-related sites have appeared on postcards including a log cabin he built for his wife. It was moved many times and regularly 'post carded' in a different location.

Still other postcards captured Grant's birthplace at Point Pleasant, Ohio near Cincinnati, and even a tree planted by Grant one 1879 date in Chicago's Washington Park. Later there were photographs of Grand and his family reproduced on postcards issued by the Ohio Historical Society which maintained the Grant Birthplace State Memorial.

Grant was born in Point Pleasant in April of 1822 where his father maintained a successful leather tanning business. Historians say Grant went unnamed for six whole weeks until his mother decided upon the name Hiram, which he grew to hate as a youngster.

When Hiram Ulysses Grant applied to West Point his name was incorrectly entered as Ulysses Simpson Grant. The Simpson part slipped in because it had been his mother's maiden name. At any rate Grant pleasantly accepted the error and never changed it from that date forward.

In 1855 Grant built a cabin on 60 acres of land near St. Louis, Missouri. It was intended as a home for himself and his new bride Julia Dent Grant. They called it Hardscrabble. The newly weds lived there only a short time before moving out in early 1856 and never returning.

Grant had an extremely successful career in the military, and during the height of the Civil War he was promoted to commander of the Union armies by President Abraham Lincoln. In April of 1865 General Grant received the surrender of General Robert E. Lee at Appomattox, Virginia to end the cruel Civil War.

By 1868 Grant was popular nationwide as a war hero and thus the natural choice as a presidential candidate. Grant was nominated by the Republican Party on the first ballot and the selection was made unanimous. He and his running mate Schuler Colfax handily won the national election that year with more than 70 percent of the electoral votes.

His first term was tarnished with scandal including attempt by some members of Grant's inner circle to corner the market on gold. The plan failed but the shadow of corruption lingered. He was re-elected however to a second term in 1872 with more than 80 percent of the electoral votes.

President Grant occupied the White House during some historical moments including when Alexander Graham Bell first transmitted the sound of the human voice on an instrument called the telephone. He was also president when General George Armstrong Custer was killed by warring Indians under the command of Sitting Bull at the Battle of Little Big Horn.

Little went well for Grant after he left office. In 1880 he was unsuccessful in an attempt to secure the Republication nomination once again for president of the United States. He won acclaim briefly however in 1883 when he was elected president of the National Rifle Association.

Grant encountered a financial disaster shortly afterwards when his investment firm collapsed and left the once national leader without funds. In 1885 Congress, aware of his near destitute state, voted to restore his previous military rank with some supplemental pay. Meanwhile Grant was critically ill but gamely penning his book Memoirs to further provide for his family.

Grant died in July of 1885 just days after the book's manuscript was completed.

He never lived to see it in print. The cause of death was throat cancer, due in part to his one time consumption of 20 cigars a day.

The late president was buried in what became Grant National Memorial. It was designed by architect John Duncan and it was dedicated by President William McKinley in 1897.

Meanwhile Grant's cabin had been sold to real estate developers in the 1890s whereupon it was disassembled and then reassembled in Webster Groves, Missouri. Next in 1903 it was sold to a coffee manufacturer for use as a promotion at the 1904 St. Louis World's Fair. Still later it was sold and moved until it became the property of the Anheuser-Bush company and restored as a public historic site.

Finally, the truly correct answer to who is buried in Grant's tomb might be twofold. Grant is buried there along with his beloved wife Julia Dent Grant.

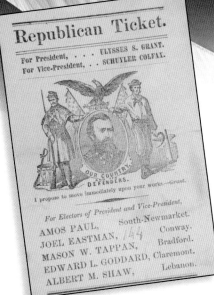

Republican Ticket for Grant and Colfax. Black on white paper. $115

Presidential Sites:
U.S. Grant Birthplace, Point Pleasant, Ohio, 513-553-4911

U.S. Grant Home State Historic Site, Galena, Illinois, 815-777-3310

Ulysses S. Grant National Historic Site, St, Louis, Missouri, 314-842-3298

President U.S. Grant. Black and white print, ca. 1890s. $5-6

U.S. Grant. Engraved print, copyright 1908 Bureau of National Literature And Art. $6-8

Eighteenth President. Beck real photo postcard. $6-8

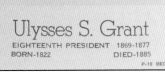

Birthplace of Grant in Cincinnati, Ohio. Leighton Co. postcard. $3-4

Gen. U.S. Grant. Grant Birthplace State Memorial postcard. $3-4

Grant's Home in Galena, Illinois. Ca. 1930s postcard. $2-3

Grant's Log Cabin, Philadelphia, Pa. Early 1900s postcard. $5-6

Souvenir of Galena, Illinois and Grant's Home. Ca. 1930s folder. $2-3

General Grant's Tomb, New York. Posted 1910. $3-4

The Grant family. Postcard based on painting by E.B. Beusell. $3-4

Home of General Grant in Galena, Illinois. Ca. 1950s postcard. $3-4

U.S. Grant and boyhood home, Georgetown, Ohio. Kraemer Art Co. postcard. Early 1900s. $3-4

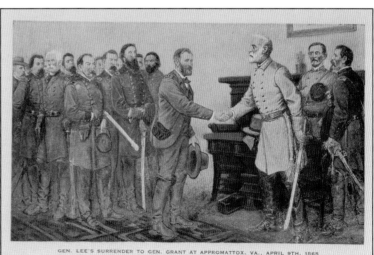

Lee's Surrender to Grant. Early 1900s postcard. $3-4

63   *Ulysses S. Grant*

Rutherford B. Hayes

President 1877 - 1881

Two centuries later historians and scholars are still debating the bizarre election of President Rutherford B. Hayes.

Ultimately the presidential election was decided by the single vote of a committee member just hours before the inauguration.

The election of 1876 had seemed simple enough. When the balloting was over New York governor Samuel Tilden, a Democrat, had won by several hundred thousand votes over Ohio governor Hayes, a Republican. The outcome of the electoral vote was however in serious doubt.

Some accounts gave Hayes 185 electoral votes compared to Tilden's 184. Controversy raged and arguments erupted across the country. Ultimately Congress decided to put together a special commission to investigate and finally decide the true results.

The commission gathering of Representatives, Senators and Supreme Court judges pondered and proceeded until shortly before the presidential inauguration. Most experts today conclude that within the confines of the commission Democrats agreed to accept Hayes if the existing Republican administration would end Reconstruction in the South. Basically this meant withdrawing federal troops in certain southern states.

As a further measure for stability Hayes was secretly given an advance oath of office in the White House on the weekend prior to the public ceremony on Monday, March 5, 1877.

Hayes was born October 4, 1822 in Delaware, Ohio. Since his father had already died before the future president was born, much of his childhood was spent with an uncle. He attended Kenyon College in Ohio before eventually going on to Harvard University.

After establishing a law practice in native Ohio, Hayes wed Lucy Webb in 1852 in Cincinnati, Ohio.

During the Civil War Hayes served as an officer in the Ohio Volunteer Army. He was wounded in the Battle of Winchester and emerged from the war effort with the rank of major general. A grateful Ohio region elected him to Congress even before his military tour was completed.

By 1867 Hayes had been elected governor of Ohio. In 1876 he attended the Republican Party's national convention in Cincinnati as Ohio's Favorite Son. To the surprise of many he was selected on the seventh ballot as his party's presidential candidate.

During the grand campaign of 1876 one of Hayes' supporters' favorite slogans was, "Hurrah for Hayes and His Honest Ways." Then came the loss of the popular vote and the victory in the Electoral College decision.

From the beginning the President and the First Lady were serious-minded people. Mrs. Hayes had been the only female student at Ohio Wesleyan University and maintained a determined personality.

The First Lady believed that the White House should be open for receptions in the evenings, no matter what the daily work schedule had been.

"These quite informal evening gatherings," wrote one observer, "where all was bright and cheerful and of good report, became the distinctive social feature of Mrs. Hayes' regime at the White House."

But all the socializing was done without liquor. Mrs. Hayes was so strict in her prohibition of alcoholic beverages and her serving lemonade instead, that she became known as Lemonade Lucy. President Hayes however maintained that the no-liquor rule in the White House was his decision. He suggested in his diaries that at least part of the reason was to appease voters who might otherwise join the political temperance party.

However the Christian Temperance Union gave full credit to Mrs. Hayes and commissioned a portrait of her which hung in the White House for decades.

It was 'Lemonade Lucy' who first brought the Easter Egg Roll to the White House. According to some accounts Congress had just passed a law closing the Capitol grounds to children rolling eggs because they were ruining the grass. Mrs. Hayes countered by opening up the White House lawn to the children and their Easter eggs.

Shortly before leaving office, President Hayes wrote to a former classmate and friend, reflecting on his White House years.

"Nobody ever left the Presidency with less regret, less disappointment, fewer heartburning, or more general content with the result of his term than I do."

From the start Hayes had declared he would serve only one term. So when that single term ended he retired to his 25-acre estate Spiegel Grove near Fremont, Ohio. He spent his final 12 years there.

Presidential Site:
Rutherford B. Hayes Presidential Center, Fremont, Ohio, 419-332-2081

President Hayes. Engraved print, copyright 1908 by Bureau of National Literature and Art. $5-6

Rutherford B. Hayes. Postcard based on painting by Morris Katz. $3-4

Rutherford Birchard Hayes. Real photo postcard. $5-6

President Hayes. Little Debbie premium card. 1992. $2-3

Rutherford B. Hayes. Colonial Bread premium card. 1976,

Christmas scene in Hayes Home. Rutherford Hayes Home and Museum photograph. Ca. 1983. $1-2

Hayes residence at Fremont, Ohio. Rutherford B. Hayes Library postcard. $2-3

James A. Garfield

President 1881

In August of 1881 President James A. Garfield dispatched a letter to assure his very worried mother regarding his health. President Garfield confided that although he had been brutally shot by an assassin, he would recover.

"Don't be disturbed by conflicting reports about my condition," President Garfield wrote his mother. "It is true I am still weak and on my back, but I am gaining every day and need only time and patience to bring me through."

Apparently the 20th president of the United States ran out of both. He died the following month.

President Garfield had briefly served in the White House at a time historically too early for the postcard era. His memorial however later established in Cleveland, Ohio was featured on many postcards. Other postcards also featured his Ohio residence, his wife Lucreita, and portraits of the late Garfield himself.

The ill-fated Garfield was born in 1831 in a place called Orange, Ohio.

Originally a school teacher, he later became a professor at a small college in Ohio. In 1858 he married a farmer's daughter, Lucretia Rudolph.

Garfield was a veteran of the Civil War and fought at Shiloh and Chickamauga. Later he returned to civilian life in Ohio and was elected to the U.S. House of Representatives.

In 1880 he was eventually nominated as a presidential candidate at the Republican National Convention. Ex-president U.S. Grant led on the first ballot, interestingly Garfield received no votes at all on the first ballot. However the nomination was Garfield's after an exhausting 36 ballots.

During the presidential election of November 1880 Garfield and vice-presidential candidate Chester Arthur edged out Democrat contender Winfield Scott and running mate William Hayden.

At some point Garfield would later quip the President "is the last person in the world to know what the people really want and think."

President Garfield could be more than candid at times in remarks. He is often quoted as stating, "ideas are the great warriors of the world, and a war that has no idea behind it is simply a brutality."

In July of 1881 Garfield was shot at a railway depot in Washington, D.C. His assassin was Charles Guiteau, a frustrated office seeker. The weapon was a .44 caliber British Bulldog revolver. After a long and lingering illness Garfield succumbed to complications arising from the gunshot wounds. He died in September of 1881 in Elberon, New Jersey. He had been moved there because physicians felt the sea air would help his recovery.

Two months later, in November of that same year, Guiteau went on trial for the murder of the president. In January of 1882 he was found guilty and was hanged at the jail in Washington D.C. the following June.

After a prolonged state funeral President Garfield was buried in Cleveland, Ohio. A substantial memorial was erected in Lakeview Cemetery eventually. It was funded by popular subscription through public donations.

Later President Garfield was featured on early 20th century postcards. They included his portrait, his wife who had served as First Lady for only seven months, his home in Mentor, Ohio, and many of his memorial structures and statues in Cleveland, Ohio.

Presidential Site:
James A. Garfield National Historic Site, Mentor, Ohio, 440-255-8722

President Garfield. Print, copyright 1908 Bureau of National Literature and Art. $4-6

James A. Garfield. Beck real photo postcard.
$6-8

President and Mrs. Garfield. Real photo postcard. $3-4

James A. Garfield Home. Ohio Natural Color Card Co.
postcard. $2-3

Home of President James Garfield. Artvue
Postcard Company postcard. $3-4

The Cincinnati Times, 1881. News of
Garfield's condition. $10-15

Garfield Home at Mentor, Ohio.
Early 1900s postcard. $3-4

James A. Garfield

President Garfield. Postcard of painting by Morris Katz. $3-4

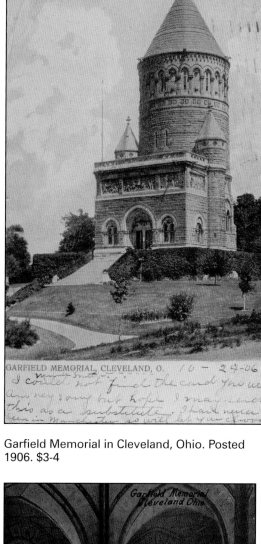

Garfield Memorial in Cleveland, Ohio. Posted 1906. $3-4

Garfield Memorial at Lake View Cemetery. Posted 1915. $3-4

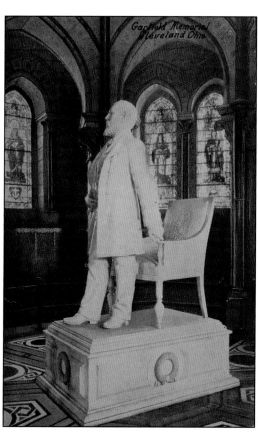

Statue at Garfield Memorial. Posted 1912. $3-4

Chester A. Arthur

President 1881 - 1885

President Chester Alan Arthur may have been somewhat controversial, but he certainly cleaned-up the White House—literally.

Arthur became president in 1881 when President James Garfield died from gunshot wounds fired by an assassin. Upon inspecting the White House residence Arthur declared:

"I will not live in a house looking this way. If Congress does not make an appropriation, I will go ahead and have it done and pay for it out of my own pocket. I will not live in a house like this."

True to his bold statement, President Arthur set up a makeshift White House in a granite mansion on Capitol Hill. By written accounts he conducted the government's business there from September to December while the White House itself was being redone by renowned artist, jeweler, and decorator Louis Comfort Tiffany.

President Arthur is said to have visited the White House each evening to investigate the results. Under his direction 24 wagon loads of furniture and other accessories were hauled away to be sold at public auction.

The person who would be the nation's 21st president was born October 5, 1830 in Fairfield, Vermont. Arthur would be the first president born in that state.

After attending public schools Arthur graduated from Union College and served for a time as teacher and as a principle. Upon completing studies in law he entered practice in New York City. Eventually he obtained a notable governmental job as Collector of the Port of New York. The position, which came by way of President U.S. Grant in 1871, offered control over considerable patronage. By 1880 he was removed from that position by President Rutherford Hayes.

His 'un-appointment' not withstanding, Arthur's name came up at the Republican Party's national convention. When James Garfield was nominated for president, some thought Arthur's addition to the ticket would appease the New York City 'crowd'. Less than a year later he would be president.

President Garfield was shot and critically wounded in July of 1881. However his death was not swift. As Garfield lay dying Arthur was summoned from New York to Washington in order to take on Presidential duties at any moment. Garfield however lingered for 80 days creating a very, very awkward situation in the White House.

After trips back and forth Arthur finally took the oath of office in his New York City residence shortly after midnight on September 18 of that year.

"Surely no more lonely and pathetic figure was ever seen assuming the powers of government," wrote a close friend later. "He had no people behind him, for Garfield, not he, was the people's choice. He had no party behind him; the dominant faction of the party hated his name—were enraged by his advancement, and distrusted his motives. He had not even his own faction behind him, for he already knew that discharge of his duties would not accord with the ardent desires of this partisanship, and that disappointment and estrangement lay before him there."

Arthur was sworn-in a second time on September 22 in the White House before members of the Cabinet and other officials.

Interestingly, President Arthur declined to hire a bodyguard and chose instead to hire a valet. And yet the previous president had been assassinated only months before. Moreover this was a time when the Secret Service's intent was mostly investigating counterfeiting and other federal crimes. Congress did not direct the Secret Service to protect the president until 1901, after still another president, President William McKinney, had been assassinated.

So it is fair to say that President Arthur put a great deal of emphasis on his appearance and his clothing.

Arthur was a widower. His wife, Ellen Herndon Arthur died in January of 1880. He became the fourth widower to enter the White House. Others up until that time were Thomas Jefferson, Andrew Jackson, and Martin Van Buren. As Arthur's only daughter was just ten years old, he asked his sister Mary Arthur McElroy to serve as mistress of the White House.

Historians credit the Arthur administration for its dramatic stand for reform, and for his untiring support of the controversial Civil Service Law. Even gifted and successful author Mark Twain told his followers, "it would be hard to better President Arthur's administration."

Leaders in his political party however did not feel that way. They rejected his efforts to seek his own presidential term. In the summer of 1884, after four ballots, the party nominated James G. Blaine rather than Arthur.

Former president Chester A. Arthur died in November of 1886 and was buried in Albany, New York.

Presidential Site:
Chester A. Arthur Historic Site, Montpelier, Vermont, 802-933-8362

Chester A. Arthur

Chester A. Arthur. Print, copyright 1908 by Bureau of National Literature and Art. $5-6

President Chester Arthur. Early 1900s postcard. $10-12

President Arthur. Little Debbie premium card. 1992. $2-3

Vice president Arthur. Real photo postcard. $3-4

Chester A. Arthur. Americana trading card. 1992. $1-2

Grover Cleveland

President 1885 - 1889
and 1893 - 1897

In historical terms Grover Cleveland had two accomplishments which remain unchallenged today.

President Cleveland was the only president to actually be married in the White House. He was also the only president to have served at two entirely different times.

Because Cleveland's two presidential terms were not consecutive, they are still an issue. The State Department has ruled that Cleveland was both the 22nd and 24th president of the United States. Other scholars disagree saying he was merely the 22nd president. More than a century later it is still being debated.

The wedding in the White House part of Cleveland's story however remains unchallenged.

Like his predecessor President James Buchanan, Cleveland arrived in the White House as a bachelor. But unlike Buchanan he left married to a charming First Lady.

The future two-time president was born March 18, 1837 in Caldwell, New Jersey. He was the fifth child in a rather large family of nine. Cleveland's father was a Presbyterian minister who named his new son Stephen Grover after a family friend. In later years Cleveland dropped his first name and went by his middle name, Grover, for the rest of his life.

Cleveland took to politics and government at an early age. He served as an assistant district attorney and sheriff of Erie County, New York. Next he was elected mayor of Buffalo, and later became governor of the New York state.

In the general election of 1884 Cleveland was nominated as a candidate president on the national Democratic Party's second ballot. After a bitter battle Cleveland narrowly defeated Republican challenger James Blaine. Out of nearly 10 million votes cast Cleveland won by around 21,000 popular votes; however he won 54 percent of the electoral vote.

The new president took the oath of office on his mother's Bible on March 4, 1885. When he was inaugurated as president he was 47 years of age.

By most all accounts Cleveland was hard working president, often laboring at his desk in the White House until 2 or 3 in the morning. It is said he spent the night reading every detail of Congressional bills. He signed over 1,000 and vetoed hundreds more.

"He sailed through American history like a steel ship loaded with monoliths of granite," wrote H. L. Mencken admiringly of Cleveland's efforts in the White House.

Then came romance.

The story of course began much earlier than Cleveland's term as president. Years earlier his law partner and dear friend Oscar Folsom was killed in a buggy accident. Cleveland became executor of Folsom's estate and seeing to the victim's widow and his 11-year-old daughter. More than a decade later when 21-year-old Frances Folsom graduated from Wells College, Cleveland wrote a letter to her suggesting that they be married.

By the time the wedding occurred Miss Folsom was 22 and Grover Cleveland was 49. They wed in the Blue Room of the White House on June 2, 1886 before a small gathering of 30 to 40 people.

Despite being the first president to be married in the White House, Cleveland lost the presidential election of 1888. Even with a larger popular vote than rival Benjamin Harrison, the Electoral College vote favored Harrison when New York and Indiana went for the Republican candidate.

In 1892 Cleveland and Harrison, like heavyweight boxers, met for a mighty rematch. This time Cleveland won decisively by more than a 500,000 popular vote margin and 62 percent of the electoral vote.

During Cleveland's second term in office Mrs. Cleveland give birth to the only child of an American president to be born within the confines of the White House. Esther Cleveland was born on September 8, 1893. She was their second daughter. Ultimately they would have five children together.

Meanwhile their older daughter Ruth played on the front lawn of the White House until too many admirers stopped to see and even hold the cute little child. Eventually she had to be hidden away from an admiring public. Sadly Ruth died at age 13 due to cerebral palsy.

By 1896 the leaders of the Democrat Party were unhappy with the Cleveland administration and chose instead William Jennings Bryan to be their presidential candidate. Bryan lost.

After leaving office for the second time, Cleveland retired to Princeton, New Jersey. He died there in 1908.

Frances Folsom Cleveland, who became the country's youngest First Lady, also became the first First Lady to re-marry. In 1913 she married a Princeton University professor.

Presidential Site:
Grover Cleveland Birthplace, Caldwell, New Jersey, 201-226-1810

Grover Cleveland. Engraved print, copyright 1908 Bureau of National Literature and Art. $6-8

Grover Cleveland. Colonial Bread premium. 1976. $2-3

Grover Cleveland. Little Debbie Cakes premium. 1992. $1-2

President Cleveland. Hand colored postcard. $10-15

Democratic Ticket. 1884 election. $105

White House wedding. Frank Leslie's Illustrated, 1886. $10-15

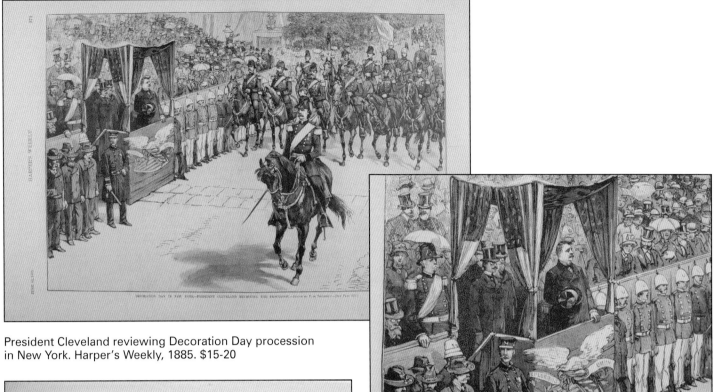

President Cleveland reviewing Decoration Day procession in New York. Harper's Weekly, 1885. $15-20

Thomas Nast drawing of President Cleveland. Harper's Weekly, 1885. $20-25

Benjamin Harrison

President 1889 - 1893

President Benjamin Harrison was known historically as the Grandfather President during the late 19th century.

For one thing he was the only grandson of a president to become president himself. For another, his second marriage produced a child actually younger than his grandchildren.

There were times during his career when Harrison's nickname was simply Grandfather's Hat.

Most of the postcards relating Harrison however came early in the 20th century after his death. Many deal with the former president's home in Indianapolis which he built himself during the 1870s. Others depict the interior of the fine old home and its vintage furniture. Still other postcards feature the Presidential portrait of Harrison or various memorial tributes to his White House service.

Harrison was born in 1833 in North Bend, Ohio. He was the fifth of his father's 13 children. And he was one of many grandchildren of former President William Henry Harrison who served briefly while Benjamin was still a youngster.

Benjamin Harrison eventually moved to Indianapolis and had a growing law practice. He failed in his campaign for governor but later became the United States Senator from Indiana.

In 1888 Harrison endured a grueling battle for the presidential nomination of the Republican Party. Among the long list of candidates was Robert Todd Lincoln the son of Abraham Lincoln and a future presidential contender named William McKinley. Harrison won on the eighth ballot.

That fall he faced incumbent President Grover Cleveland. One of the pro-Harrison campaign jingles that year went as follows:

Steamboat coming 'round the bend;

Goodbye, old Grover, goodbye.

Filled up full with Harrison's men,

Goodbye, old Grover, goodbye!

Whether it was the jingle or a dozen other things, Harrison was able to defeat Cleveland. While Cleveland narrowly won the popular vote, Harrison captured a decisive margin in the Electoral College.

The 55-year-old Harrison took office in March of 1889. Accounts say that more than 12,000 crowded into the Pension Office in Washington, D.C. to party after the inauguration. An orchestra of 100 provided the dance tunes.

Harrison's term in office was not particularly earth-shaking. However there were more states admitted to the Union during his presidency than any time in history. Welcomed to the U.S. were South Dakota, North Dakota, Montana, Washington, Idaho, and Wyoming. A record not likely to ever be broken unless this country would annex Mexico, Cuba and much of Central America.

During the presidency Harrison remained married to his first wife Caroline Lavinia Scott Harrison. However Mrs. Harrison became ill while living at the White House and was attended by her niece Mary Scott Lord Dimmick. It was said that Mary Scott also took charge of many social functions at the White House on behalf of the ailing Mrs. Harrison.

Mrs. Harrison died before her husband's term ended. In 1892 Harrison lost a political rematch to Grover Cleveland. Afterwards Harrison returned to a law practice in Indianapolis. He soon married his second wife, Mary Scott Lord Dimmick.

Mary gave birth to a baby daughter in 1897. The new arrival made the child younger that Harrison's four grandchildren. His first wife Caroline had given birth to a son and daughter. Each of them had two children, the last of which was born in 1896.

Benjamin Harrison died in March of 1901 in the Indianapolis home where he had lived for so many years. Inside were most of the original furniture plus other gifts acquired during his White House years. One example was a horn chair given by a Texas resident during Harrison's trip across the United States. There was also a gold headed cane from a Wisconsin supporter with Harrison's name etched in diamonds. All were later the object of postcards.

President Harrison died at age 67 and was the first President to succumb in the 20th century. He was buried at Crown Hill Cemetery in Indianapolis.

Presidential Site:
President Benjamin Harrison Home, Indianapolis, Indiana, 317-631-1889

Benjamin Harrison. Postcard of portrait by Morris Katz.
$3-4

Benjamin Harrison and Mrs. Harrison. Real photo
postcard. $3-4

Benjamin Harrison, 23rd president. Real photo postcard. $3-4

President Benjamin Harrison. Postcard based on portrait at the
Benjamin Harrison Memorial Home in Indianapolis, Indiana. $3-4

Benjamin Harrison

Residence of Benjamin
Harrison in Indianapolis,
Indiana. Posted in 1907.
$5-6

Front Hall of
Harrison home
in Indianapolis,
Indiana. W. W. Cline
Co. postcard. $2-3

23

Benjamin Harrison
1889-1893

Born: August 20, 1833
Died: March 13, 1901
Party: Republican
Home State: IN
Occupation: Lawyer
VP: Levi P. Morton
Notable Event: Sherman Anti-Trust Act
Fun Fact: Most states admitted during his term (6)

Little Debbie
Snack Cakes

Benjamin Harrison monument
in Indianapolis, Indiana.
Majestic Publishing postcard.
$3-4

Benjamin Harrison. Little Debbie
Cakes premium card. 1993. $1-3

William McKinley

President 1897 - 1901

President William McKinley was tragically assassinated early in the 20th century just as the era of the postcard was dawning. The timing of the national misfortune was grimly perfect for the country's production of curious postcards.

For a decade after his death President McKinley's image and those images relating to his death were extensively featured on everything from official U.S. government postal cards to memorial postcards used by the McKinley Club itself.

Twice elected to the presidency, McKinley had endeared himself to the public with the campaign of 1896. After receiving the Republican Party's nomination McKinley more or less retired to his home in Canton, Ohio. While Democrat challenger William Jennings Bryan toured to the country and spoke to millions, McKinley conducted what historians now call his "front porch campaign".

Basically the presidential candidate spoke to the party faithful by reading speeches and shaking hands in his front yard. McKinley also became the first presidential candidate to use the telephone for campaigning purposes. Reportedly he regularly telephoned some 30 or 40 campaign managers in various states. The strategy worked and McKinley won election by an overwhelming margin.

McKinley won re-election in 1900 defeating Bryan and Prohibition candidate John Wooley.

On September 6, 1901 the ill-fated President was attending a public reception at the Pan-American Exposition in Buffalo, New York. McKinley greeted guests at the Milburn residence located at 1168 Delaware Avenue. Shortly after 4 p.m. Leon Czolgosz, a disgruntled factory and self-proclaimed anarchist neared the President. Using a revolver hidden in his handkerchief, Czolgosz shot McKinley twice.

Immediately boarding a special train vice president Theodore Roosevelt was rushed to the site where he was assured the President's life was not in danger. Relieved, the vice president then rejoined his family vacationing in the Adirondack Mountains.

Short days later the President's condition worsened. The vice president was notified this time by special courier and again boarded a special train, rushing to Buffalo. Before Roosevelt could arrive at the Milburn house, on September 14 McKinley died. Within hours of Roosevelt's arrival he was administered the oath of office.

Ironically McKinley would briefly lay in state at the same location of the exposition reception and the assassination- the Milburn house. Later the home was featured on numerous postcards.

Justice was swift. The assassin Czolgosz was convicted of the crime of murder after a trial which lasted little more than eight hours. Czolgosz was electrocuted at Auburn State Prison on October 29, 1901. The execution had taken place just 54 days after the shooting of the President, and just 45 days following McKinley's actual death.

Just a year later the Sears, Roebuck and Company catalog- of all places- offered readers a slide show collection of events surrounding the assassination. The set of 15 slides, assured the catalog, "are proving the most attractive of special lecture features ever offered."

The so-called special lecture features sold by Sears amounted to various slides which could be shown to the public via a stereopticon. The device provided near-stereographic three-dimensional image.

Included in the McKinley Assassination set were "realistic views of the assassination, the assassin taken within ten minutes of his capture by police, and beautiful illustrations of the funeral cortege (funeral procession). In fact, a complete illustrated history of the most terrible tragedy of the present century."

The Sears sales pitch was that by combining the slides and the stereopticon an enterprising person could earn a nice income by traveling around and charging admission for 'lecture programs' on topics such as the assassination of President McKinley.

Indeed President McKinley was the first president to be assassinated in the 20th century. Previously the 19th century had witnessed the assassination of both Abraham Lincoln and James Garfield.

By 1903 McKinley was memorialized with his image on the official postal card of the U.S. government. The oval picture of the late President appeared beneath the postage one cent line. Beneath it was 1843-McKinley-1901.

Commercial postcards were more prolific. There were several versions of the Milburn house. Others depicted the public square draped in mourning at Cleveland, Ohio. Additionally there were views of the Ohio state capital in Columbus and views of McKinley's hometown in Canton. Many, seeing the public's fascination with the sensational topic, made reference to the assassination.

Even after death McKinley had a strong following, as witnessed by various McKinley clubs

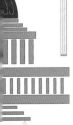

which sprang up around the country. A favorite of the clubs were commemorative postcards depicting the late President and perhaps a favored quotation.

In 1908 the Scofield-Pierson Company of Indianapolis produced such a color tinted postcard. Below the McKinley quote, "God's will, not ours, be done," was a small bouquet of carnations. The carnation was the state flower of McKinley's native Ohio, and it was said he regularly wore one in the lapel of his coat for good luck.

Such a postcard was mailed to members of a particular McKinley club in 1911.

A printed message on its reverse read in part:

"As the birthday of our beloved martyred President, William McKinley, January 29, occurs this year on Sunday, the McKinley Club will observe said anniversary on Monday evening January 30, as a tribute to him whose public services and kindly disposition ever remains as one of sweetest memory.

"The Hon. A. M. Hall will make the address. Wear a pink carnation. In loving remembrance. McKinley Club."

It was posted Jan. 27, 1911, two days before the late President's birthday. McKinley typically wore a red carnation in his lapel for good luck. It was the state flower of his native Ohio.

Presidential Sites:
McKinley Museum and National Memorial, Canton, Ohio, 330-455-7043
McKinley Memorial Library & Museum, Niles, Ohio, 330-652-1704

William McKinley. Copyright 1900 print from Orations Vol. Eight. $3-4

Postcard of painting by Morris Katz. Dated 1967. $5-6

Public Square in Cleveland, Ohio. Draped in mourning after President McKinley died. Early 1900s postcard. $5-10

McKinley Shot at Buffalo. Columbus Evening Dispatch, 1901. $25

The President Twice Shot. *The Los Angles Times*. $25

William McKinley campaign card. Ca. 1900. $25-30

McKinley Memorial in Columbus, Ohio. Posted 1908. $3-4

Left: Niles High School at Niles, Ohio. McKinley Memorial Museum postcard, $5-10

79

William McKinley

McKinley's Birthplace at McKinley Heights. Posted 1934. $5-6

Where Pres. McKinley Died. Posted 1913. $5-6

The Milburn Residence. Posted 1905. $5-6

McKinley's Birthplace at Riverside Park. McKinley's Birthplace Memorial postcard. $4-5

Tomb of President McKinley In Canton, Ohio. Posted 1906. $3-4

William McKinley. Little Debbie premium card. 1993. $2-3

McKinley Monument in Canton, Ohio. Ca. 1950s postcard. $2-3

Theodore Roosevelt

President 1901 - 1909

President "Teddy" Roosevelt championed the pioneer spirit at the onset of the 20th century. He was the first president to ride in an automobile. He was also the first American president to fly in an airplane.

Then too TR was the first president to inspire a stuffed toy which still fondly bares his name today. Roosevelt was also the first president to win the Nobel Peace prize. He was also the first to be presidential candidate for two major political parties.

Theodore Roosevelt, who would become the 26th president of the United States, was born during 1858 in New York City.

Triumph and tragedy followed Roosevelt in the early years of his career. In 1884 both his mother and wife, Alice Hathaway Roosevelt, died on the same day. That same year TR's permanent home was completed at Sagamore Hills on Oyster Bay in Long Island. It was named for the Indian chieftain Sagamore Mohannis and was constructed at a cost of $16,975.

TR became a national hero while serving in the military during the Spanish-American War of 1898. Back at home, the public cheered the daring efforts of Roosevelt and his Roosevelt Rough Riders during that conflict.

Late in the 19th century the voters of New York State elected TR governor by a large margin. While still a relatively young man Roosevelt was nominated as the Republican vice presidential candidate in 1900. GOP presidential nominee William McKinley and Roosevelt were a sweep into the White House that year.

Teddy Roosevelt might have spent the rest of his political career in the relative obscurity of the vice presidency had not tragedy struck President McKinley. In September 1901 while visiting the Pan American Exposition, McKinley was shot and fatally wounded by a factory worker. After lingering for several days McKinley died and Roosevelt took the oath of office on Saturday afternoon.

At age 42 TR was the youngest person ever to hold the office of U.S. President. Wrote the Saturday Evening Post shortly afterwards:

"Under the shadow a heavy sorrow the Nation greets President Roosevelt." His youth and the national 'sorrow' not withstanding, Roosevelt rapidly rose to the responsibility of the high office."

At some point in his presidency the sportsman-hunter Roosevelt was widely credited with sparing a bear cub during a hunting exposition in a southern state. TR reportedly refused to shoot the animal and an editorial cartoon depicting the noble deed attracted nationwide acclaim. It also prompted the production and sale of a series of stuffed animals which quickly became known as 'teddy bears.' The name endures.

In 1902 Roosevelt became the first president to ride in an automobile. He made the historic trip in a Columbia Electric Victoria. Two years later TR was nominated for president in his own right by the Republican national convention. In November he defeated the Democrat nominee Alton Parker by two and a half million votes, capturing more than 70 percent of the electoral votes.

During the final year of his White House term the ruling Republican Party became divided into two factions—a conservative wing and a progressive wing. Roosevelt helped William Howard Taft secure the GOP nomination. Taft also won the general election in 1908, but disagreements continued.

Roosevelt had a brush with aviation history in October of 1910. He was a passenger in an airplane flown by Archie Hoxsey aboard a type B pusher plane. The craft itself had been built by the now famous Wright Brothers. Ironically TR had been president in 1903 when the same Wrights first flew at Kitty Hawk, North Carolina. On the Roosevelt flight the plane climbed to an altitude of 50 feet before leveling off. The entire airborne event lasted about four minutes above the Aviation Field in St. Louis, Missouri.

The former president turned to politics again in 1912, when he again sought the Republican Party's nomination for president. The bid however was rejected and a bitter Roosevelt left the party and formed his own Progressive Party. It was nicknamed the Bull Moose Party in a nod to Roosevelt's robust health and avid interest in the out doors.

It was a fascinating three-way presidential race and ended up in defeat for both the Progressives and the Republicans. Democrat Woodrow Wilson was the victor thanks in a large part to the Roosevelt-Republican division.

For the most part following that campaign Roosevelt retired to private life at his beloved Sagamore Hills.

Shortly before his untimely death TR is reportedly to have commented to his wife, "I wonder if you will ever know how I love Sagamore Hill?"

Roosevelt died unexpectedly of a heart attack in 1919. He was buried near his Oyster Bay home at Young's Memorial Cemetery.

Presidential Sites:
Theodore Roosevelt Birthplace National Historic Site, New York, New York, 212-260-1616
Theodore Roosevelt Inaugural National Historic Site, Buffalo, New York, 716-884-0095
Sagamore Hill National Historic Site, Oyster Bay, New York, 516-922-4788

It Was A Famous Victory. *Los Angeles Times* newspaper, November, 1904. $50

Theodore Roosevelt. Rotograph Series postcard, dated 1904. $8-10

President Roosevelt in Indianapolis. Posted 1907. $15-20

"Our President." Advertising supplement, ca. 1900s. $4-5

President Roosevelt. Signed photograph, dated 1906. $220 (Skinner Inc.)

Theodore Roosevelt. Little Debbie premium card. 1993. $1-2

Roosevelt in bi-plane. Real photo postcard, date 1910. *Courtesy of Swan Galleries*. $200 (rare)

Badlands Ranch of Theodore Roosevelt. North Dakota Scenes postcard. $2-3

Sagamore Hill in Long Island, New York. Postcard view of drawing room at Roosevelt residence. $2-3

Theodore Roosevelt

William H. Taft

President 1909 - 1913

Ohio native son William Howard Taft was not the first American president to be featured on postcards.

However the rotund Taft did accomplish many 'firsts' as the country's 27th president. He was the first president to throw the opening pitch at a major league baseball game, the first to reign over 48 states, and the first to weigh over 300 pounds.

William Howard Taft was born during the year 1857 to Alphonso and Louise Taft in Cincinnati, Ohio. Taft's father had earlier served with distinction as Attorney General and as Secretary of War under President U.S. Grant.

After a successful career as a lawyer and federal judge, Taft like his father went on to Presidential service. Under President Teddy Roosevelt he served in many capacities including governor of the Philippines and a member of the cabinet.

In 1908 Taft was practically hand-picked by Roosevelt to succeed him as president. Not surprisingly Taft was nominated on the first ballot at the Republican National Convention.

During the presidential campaign even Taft's campaign songs made reference to his enormous girth. Among them, "Get on the Raft For Taft," and "Get in Line for Big Bill Taft."

'Big Bill' tipping the scales somewhere between 330 pounds and 350 pounds- depending upon which account one chose to believe- defeated Democrat William Jennings Bryant handily in that 1908 national election.

A howling blizzard in March of 1909 forced the outdoor ceremonies of Taft's inauguration to be held in the Capitol building instead. Oddly retiring President Roosevelt left Washington by train without taking part in the event.

During Taft's term the 16th amendment granting income taxing power to the Federal government was passed by Congress. During his tenure Arizona and New Mexico became states of the Union, making the Taft the first president of fully 48 states.

Outside the White House great numbers of Japanese cherry trees were planted while Taft was in office. Inside the White House a four-man bathtub was installed to accommodate the huge frame of the president. One account in the Saturday Evening Post indicated that Taft had previously become trapped in the regular-sized tub and required assistance to free his self.

For sports fans his most note worthy accomplishment may have been pitching out the first ball at a major league baseball game. Taft was the first president to make such a pitch. It occurred April 14, 1910 at the American League opener between Washington and Philadelphia.

While a resident of the White House, President Taft spent part of his off-duty time at his spacious Summer Home in Beverly, Massachusetts. The summer place was sometimes illustrated on postcards, including one posted in 1910. The sender penciled on the reverse, "This place is four miles from Salem. I have quite a collection of cards."

Such a postcard would fall in the contemporaneous category as it was posted while Taft was still in office and still sometimes using the summertime residence. There is some indication however that Taft may have been happier 'on vacation' than on the job. In 1911 he reportedly confided to this brother Charles, "I am not very happy in this re-nomination and re-election business. I have set my teeth and go through with it… But I shall be willing to retire and let another take the burden."

That 'another' may have been his former friend and mentor Teddy Roosevelt. The two had a major falling out when Taft was nominated as president at the Republication National Convention in 1912, and Roosevelt walked out. The ex-president then headed his own Progressive Party. It was nicknamed the Bull Moose Party as a tribute to Roosevelt's own robust health.

The fallout and the third party effort meant disaster for William Howard Taft. In the general election that year he eked out only 23 percent of the popular vote. Roosevelt did somewhat better but both lost to Democrat Woodrow Wilson.

Afterwards Taft returned to his home in Cincinnati but his life in public service was far from over.

In 1921 President Warren G. Harding appointed Taft to the United States Supreme Court. Thus he became the first American president to serve in the high court. He served on the Supreme Court before resigning due to ill health.

Taft died in March of 1930, at age 72. He was the first president to be buried at Arlington National Cemetery in Arlington, Virginia.

Uniquely, Taft was the only person in America to ever serve in both the executive branch and the judicial branch of the Federal government.

Presidential Site:

William Howard Taft National Historic Site, Cincinnati, Ohio, 513-684-3262

Sweeping Victory For Taft And Prosperity. *Los Angeles Times* newspaper, 1908. $50

William H. Taft

TWENTY-SEVENTH PRESIDENT 1909-1913
BORN-1857   DIED-1930

P-26 BECK

William H. Taft. Beck postcard. $5-6

Wm H. Taft. Early 1900s postcard. $2-3

New England States Are For Taft

Chicago Tribune Poll Shows that Taft is overwhelmingly the choice of New England Republicans for the Presidency as he is of Middle West Republicans

RECAPITULATION OF THE TRIBUNE'S NEW ENGLAND BALLOT ON THE PRESIDENCY

STATES	Do you approve the progressive policies of the president? Yes	No	Do you prefer a candidate of progressive or conservative schools? Progressive	Conservative	Not Voting	Cannon 1st Choice	2d Choice	Fairbanks 1st Choice	2d Choice	Knox 1st Choice	2d Choice	Hughes 1st Choice	2d Choice	TAFT 1st Choice	2d Choice	3d Choice	OTHER CANDIDATES Roosevelt	Knot	Crane	Cortelyou	Foraker
Massachusetts	100	12	3	81	12	2	9	12	1	4	2	6	15	30	42	1	56	22	4	17	6	6	1	1
New Hampshire	70	9	4	70	10	1	2	7	11	3	9	1	6	16	35	11	50	10	3	20	3		2
Connecticut	65	16	1	58	18	4	3	10	2	9	10	1	6	12	14	35	13	53	17	2	11	4	2
Vermont	110	17	2	96	24	4	9	26	1	6	20	47	49	11	61	32	10	28	6
Rhode Island	18	2		12	3	1		1		2	11	11	2		2	2
Maine	80	11	2	72	17	3	9	11	1	8	12	1	30	31	58	19	4	16	1
Total	443	67	12	389	94	37	15	35	77	8	40	56	6	28	70	139	211	4	289	102	23	94	19	8	4	3

¶ Taft is pre-eminently the first choice of the Republicans of every one of these six New England States.
¶ TAFT RECEIVED MORE VOTES THAN ALL THE OTHER CANDIDATES TOGETHER.
¶ Taft is the second choice of 83 out of 94 Republicans who named Roosevelt as their first choice making him in reality the first choice of 372 out of 520.
¶ This means the solid New England vote of 52 for Taft in the National Convention.
¶ ANALAYZE THESE FIGURES!
¶ AND REMEMBER THE MIDDLE WEST!
¶ AND WATCH FOR WHAT COMES NEXT!

New England States Are For Taft. Campaign postcard. $6-8

Summer home in
Beverly, Mass. Posted
1910. $4-5

PRESIDENT TAFT'S SUMMER HOME, BEVERLY, MASS.

INAUGURAL PARADE, LOOKING UP 15TH STREET, WASHINGTON, D.C.

Inaugural parade
of President Taft.
Ottenheimer
postcard. $8-10

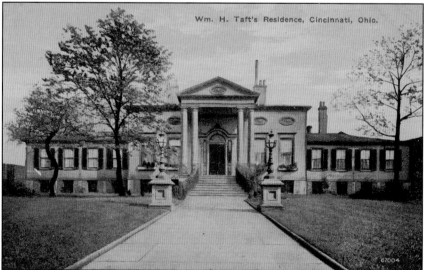

Wm. H. Taft's Residence, Cincinnati, Ohio.

Taft residence in Cincinnati, Ohio.
Early 1900s postcard. $2-3

27

William H. Taft
1909-1913
Born: September 15, 1857
Died: March 8, 1930
Party: Republican
Home State: OH
Occupation: Lawyer
VP: James S. Sherman
Notable Event: Income Tax Amendment ratified
Fun Fact: First to keep an auto at the White House

Little Debbie
Snack Cakes

William H. Taft. Little Debbie
premium card. 1992. $1-2

Woodrow Wilson

President 1913 - 1921

America's 28th president, Woodrow Wilson, was featured on postcards both as a presidential candidate and later when his residences were tourist sites.

In less than three years Wilson went from private citizen to President of the United States. That transformation is still a record nearly a century later.

It went like this.

Although a distinguished educator Wilson had never held public office in 1910 when he was nominated by the Democrat party for governor of New Jersey. He had held that office for only two years when he was nominated and elected president.

Of course there were some obstacles along the way.

As president of Princeton University he was not the overwhelming favorite at the Democrat National Convention. As a matter of fact it took 46 ballots to capture the nomination.

The Republican National Convention nominated William Taft of Ohio. Former president Theodore Roosevelt meanwhile bolted the GOP to accept the nomination of the Progressive Party. Roosevelt compared his strength to that of a bull moose, and thus the movement coined the phrase Bull Moose Party.

As a result the 1912 campaign was a three-way affair. When it was over Wilson won by two million votes. Moreover he captured more than 80 percent of the electoral vote. Roosevelt came in second place. Taft, winning only in Utah and Vermont, came in a distant third.

And historically Wilson became the first person to meet and defeat two other American presidents in a single election.

By March of 1913 Wilson occupied the White House. The entire sidewalk to oval office trip had taken just two years and 170 days.

Tragically President Wilson's first wife, Ellen Axson Wilson, died during his first term in office. The following year in 1915 President Wilson married the widow Edith Galt.

In 1916 Wilson was again nominated for president by the Democrat party. His Republican party rival that year was Charles Hughes of New York. Wilson won the presidency again, but this time by a much narrower margin of around 600,000 votes. Wilson's image had appeared on postcards during that particular campaign effort, usually they were quite colorful examples.

The United States, under Wilson's leadership, declared war on Germany in 1917. Its was also noted that as a wartime gesture Wilson rode to Sunday church in a horse-draw carriage, and a flock of sheep were allowed to graze on the White House lawn. It was during that same year that a feisty Wilson denounced opposing political leaders in Washington as "a little group of willful men, representative of no opinion but their own, (who) have rendered the great government of the United States helpless and contemptible."

While the war ended in 1918, the nation's war against the sale and manufacture of liquor was still very much underway. The 18th amendment to the constitution was passed early in 1919, and it became the beginning of an era known as Prohibition.

Unfortunately that same year President Wilson suffered a stroke and never fully recovered. He died in March of 1921 shortly after the inauguration of President Warren Harding.

Wilson was buried in the National Cathedral, at the time the only president to actually be buried in Washington, D.C.

Edith Wilson, the president's second wife, lived long enough to attend the inauguration of President John Kennedy in 1961. She died later that same year.

Over the years Wilson was featured on a number of postcards of his homes which have become tourist attractions. He was born in Staunton, Virginia; then soon moved to Augusta, Georgia; and while still a youngster also lived in Columbia, South Carolina. All three locations memorialized him with later postcards, as did other sites including the National Cathedral.

Presidential Sites:
Woodrow Wilson Birthplace and Museum, Staunton, Virginia, 703-885-0897
Woodrow Wilson House, Washington, District of Columbia, 202-387-4062

Wilson Carries California. *Los Angeles Times* newspaper, 1916. $45

Taking Oath of Office. Ottenheimer postcard. 1917. $5-6

The President and Mrs. Wilson. Garrison Inc. postcard. $6-8

Woodrow Wilson's Presidential Limousine. Postcard of 1919 Pierce-Arrow. Issued by Woodrow Wilson Presidential Library and Museum

Twenty-Eighth President. Beck real photo postcard. $6-8

The flag he loves... Patriotic postcard. Posted 1918. $6-8

President Woodrow Wilson. Postcard based on portrait by F. Graham Coates. Issued by Woodrow Wilson Presidential Library and Museum

Birthplace in Staunton, Virginia. Ashville Post Card Co. postcard. $2-3

Wilson's home and memorial in Columbia, South Carolina. Posted in 1938. $2-3

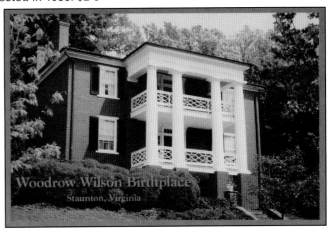

Boyhood home in Columbia, South Carolina. Early 1900s postcard. $2-4

Woodrow Wilson Birthplace in Staunton, Virginia. Official postcard Issued by Woodrow Wilson Presidential Library and Museum

Boyhood home at Augusta, Georgia. Posted in 1949. $2-3

Woodrow Wilson Passes Away. *New York Times* newspaper, 1924. $45

Victory Greetings. Patriotic postcard. $10-15

Woodrow Wilson

Warren G. Harding

President 1921 - 1923

During the presidential campaign of 1920, Warren G. Harding was featured on some postcards.

Harding, a veteran Ohio printer and newspaper editor, was one of the last presidential aspirants to confine his campaign almost entirely to the print media. Ironically both Harding and his rival James Cox had print media backgrounds. Harding was editor and publisher of the Marion (Ohio) Star. Cox was the owner and publisher of the Dayton (Ohio) Daily News.

Radio remained a relatively obscure medium during that presidential campaign. In fact it was the first time in history that presidential election returns were broadcast on radio.

During the campaign Harding lived in a fashionable home at 380 Mount Avenue in Marion, Ohio. The attractive nine-room structure, built in 1891, was home for Harding and his wife Florence Kling DeWolfe Harding until they literally moved into the White House.

Later that fine home was restored by the Harding Memorial Association and featured on a variety of promotional postcards.

Harding, America's 29th president was born near Corsica, Ohio the same year that the Civil War ended. It turned out to be a large family, Warren Gamaliel was the first of eight children. Harding grew up in the Buckeye state, attended school there and participated in the usual school activities including band. Historically he was the first band member to be elected President of the United States.

As a United States senator from Ohio, Harding was nominated on the tenth ballot of the Republican national convention in the summer of 1920. His running mate turned out to be Calvin Coolidge.

From the start he urged a return "to normalcy" from the ravages of World War I "to steady a civilization which has been fevered by the supreme upheaval of all the world."

During a speech in Boston that year, Harding dramatically called for "healing and not heroics, not surgery but serenity, not submergence in internationality, but sustainment in triumphant nationality."

As Harding sought votes that year, one of his campaign theme songs was, "Harding You're the Man For Us." It was written by entertainer and the star of the first talking motion picture Al Jolson. Something must have helped; Harding effectively carried 37 of the then 48 states against Cox and his vice presidential candidate Franklin Roosevelt.

Harding took the oath of office in March of 1921. Among other things he became the first president to ride to the inaugural ceremony in an automobile.

Still another first for President Harding proved to be tragic. In August of 1923 Harding became the first American president to journey to Alaska. Unfortunately he became ill on that trip and died during a stop-over in San Francisco.

Most school students who study that period of American history are reminded of Harding and the so-called Teapot Dome scandal. The Teapot Dome was actually an oil reserve in Wyoming. Harding's Secretary of Interior and Attorney General were accused of accepting bribes in connection with the leasing of its oil reserves to private companies. Harding was not directly implicated in the scheme but bore the stain of it.

Following Harding's death the Harding Memorial Association raised $783,000 in public subscriptions to construct a giant memorial to him. Located in Marion, Ohio and made of Georgian marble, it rose 52 feet and was 108 feet in diameter. It too was featured on a number of postcards.

Presidential Site:

Harding Home and Museum, Marion, Ohio, 614-387-9630

Right:
President Warren G. Harding. Genuine Photograph postcard.
$5-6

Harding and Shortridge Win. *Los Angeles Times* extra, 1920. $45

Harding Wins; Million Lead Here. *New York Times*, 1920. $45

President's Body to Lie in State. *Columbus Evening Dispatch*, 1923. $30

Harding Candidate for President. Real photo postcard. $3-4

Harding, Printer and Publisher. Harding Memorial Association postcard. $5-6

Warren G. Harding, Printer and Publisher

Warren G. Harding

President Harding Playing Golf.
Genuine Photograph postcard. $6-8

Sincerely Yours....Artvue Postcard Co.
postcard. $3-4

Warren G. Harding. Americana trading
card. 1992. $1-2

Harding Home. Harding Memorial Association postcard. $2-3

Harding Home library. Harding Memorial Association
postcard. $2-3

Harding Memorial
in Marion, Ohio.
Harding Home and
Museum postcard.
$4-5

Calvin Coolidge

President 1923 - 1929

President Calvin Coolidge served the nation during the Roaring Twenties and appeared on a fair share of postcards during that decade and later.

Sometimes called "Silent Cal" for his quiet demeanor, Coolidge was never the less articulate and highly regarded as a leader throughout his White House years.

Coolidge was the first president to be literally born on the Fourth of July. He was born July 4, 1872 in Plymouth, Vermont. That year marked only the 96th anniversary of the nation's Declaration of Independence.

After holding various public offices, Coolidge became governor of the state of Massachusetts in 1919. He gained national fame when as governor he summoned the National Guard to quell the Boston police strike. At the time he was said to have uttered his most notable quote:

"There is no right to strike against public safety by anybody, anytime, anywhere."

The following year Coolidge was nominated as the Republican vice presidential candidate to run with Warren Harding. In early 1921 Coolidge and his wife Grace left their fashionable home on Massasoit Street in Northampton which they had rented for $28 a month, and moved to Washington.

When President Harding died in August of 1923, Coolidge suddenly assumed the powerful office of the presidency. Historic accounts say the new president took the oath of office from his father by the light of a kerosene lamp in the wee hours of the morning.

By the general election of 1924 Coolidge was near the height of his popularity. At the Republican national convention that year he was nominated by the party on the very first ballot. The Democrats meanwhile amassed more than 100 ballots before finally selecting John Davis from among a long list of some 60 candidates.

Coolidge handily won the general election that year capturing more than 70 percent of the electoral vote.

Compared to many other presidents before and afterward, Coolidge's term in office might be considered relatively uneventful. He signed an immigration bill in 1924 reducing quotas established a few years earlier. He also signed a bill granting citizenship to then non-citizen Native American Indians born in the United States.

The diesel electric locomotive was placed in service during his White House years, and the nation's first woman governor was elected in Wyoming—Nellie Ross.

'Silent Cal' was known to frequently enjoy a good cigar in the White House. For exercise he daily rode an electric horse which he had installed in his White House bedroom.

During the 1920s a scattering of postcards depicted Coolidge addressing the United States Congress, and his former home in Massachusetts. Other postcards featured the site where he was born, his school, and his early church.

Coolidge surprised his party and much of the nation with is decision not to seek re-election in the 1928 contest. Instead he and his wife returned to private life and their home in Northampton, Mass.

Those who might not recall this particular president might recall the remarkable concrete structure named in his honor. Coolidge Dam was constructed starting in 1928 as a major source of water control and power supply in the West.

Years after his presidency, Coolidge was still actively engaged in commentary on national affairs. In 1932 he wrote in the Saturday Evening Post, "the only permanent remedy, the only relief for higher taxes, is a reduction of public expenditures."

The former president died in January of 1933. He is buried in Notch Cemetery in Plymouth Notch, Vermont. Along side him is his son Calvin Junior who died at age 16 while Coolidge was still serving in the White House.

Presidential Site:
Calvin Coolidge Memorial Foundation, Inc., Plymouth, Vermont, 802-672-3389

Harding Dies; Calvin Coolidge Is President. *The Los Angeles Times*, 1923. $35

Calvin Coolidge. Colonial Bread premium card. 1976. $2-3

Grace Coolidge. Postcard based on portrait by Howard Chandler Christy. $3-4

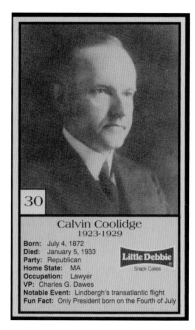

Calvin Coolidge. Little Debbie premium card. 1993. $1-3

President Coolidge addressing Congress. Ca. 1920s postcard. $4-5

Coolidge Home in Northampton, Mass. Ca. 1920s postcard. $3-4

Coolidge Does Not Choose To Run. *Columbus Dispatch* newspaper, 1927. $30

Calvin Coolidge born in Plymouth, Vermont. Hughes & Co. postcard. $3-4

Cemetery in Plymouth, Vermont. Real photo postcard. $3-4

Herbert Hoover

Possibly the most intriguing of all post-cards related to former President Herbert Hoover was the real photo postcard depicting him and former President Harry Truman.

The unique image came from the dedication of the Hoover Presidential Library in 1962. Both were aging elder statesmen who had long been friends despite differences and representing different political parties.

According to some accounts the friendship between Hoover and Truman had begun around 1945.

On the reverse of the real photo postcard was the following message:

"Mutual respect and admiration outweighed the difference of political party. Hoover asked Truman to be his guest at the dedication of the Hoover Presidential Library in 1962. The two ex-Presidents were photographed on that occasion at the display of Hoover's presidential office."

Other Hoover postcards included the president's birthplace in West Branch, Iowa. Still others included his wife Mrs. Lou Henry Hoover.

Hoover was born August 10, 1874 in West Branch. His wife-to-be was born in Waterloo, Iowa. Both later attended Stanford University in California where they met. The couple married in 1899 one year after Mrs. Hoover graduated from Stanford.

During the 1920s Hoover served as secretary of commerce under both President Warren Harding and later President Calvin Coolidge.

In the summer of 1928 Hoover was nominated as a candidate for President by the Republican national convention. Meeting in Kansas City the GOP selected Hoover on the first ballot. Later in the summer Democrats nominated Al Smith of New York as his opponent in that race.

To this day historians disagree over the memorable campaign regarding "a chicken in every pot." Some attribute it to Hoover, some attribute to his opponent Smith in 1928, and others claim it did not become lexicon until the campaign four years later.

Television came into play for the first time in a presidential election. However it was Al Smith and not Hubert Hoover who appeared on the scene. Smith's presidential nomination notification ceremony was televised from Albany, New York. TV pictures were transmitted and sent out by short wave through the facilities of the General Electric Company.

That November Hoover and vice president candidate Charles Curtis won handily over Smith and Democrat vice president choice Joseph Rob-

inson. A crowd of some 50,000 watched Hoover take his oath of office in March of 1929. Despite the rain, the dirigible Los Angeles, four blimps, and 30 planes flew over Washington, D.C. to mark the occasion.

During his presidential term the Star Spangled Banner was officially adopted as the national anthem and Amelia Earhart Putnam became the first woman to complete a transatlantic solo flight. In July of 1932 the so-called bonus army march of unemployed veterans took place in Washington. After living briefly in makeshift shacks they were dispatched by federal troops.

The bonus army debacle and the economic debacle of the Great Depression contributed to a major decline in the popularity of Hoover. Ironically it was Hoover himself who actually coined the word "depression" in reference to the economic downturn of that era.

The following November Hoover was defeated in his bid for re-election by Democrat candidate Franklin Delano Roosevelt.

Hoover spent some of his post-administration years in a plush home at 623 Mirada Avenue in Palo Alto, California. The mansion stood atop San Juan Hill on the Stanford University Campus in Santa Clara Valley. Decades later it became a major tourist attraction.

Although Hoover more or less retired to private life, it wasn't total. In the book Mr. President, historian Charles A. Beard noted, "after a season of silence, Hoover began to dispatch messages to the nation from his Palo Alto home on liberty and the mission of the Republican Party."

During his lifetime the Hoover name was linked to both miserable and mighty structures. As a result of the bonus army's march the squalor of huts occupied by the veterans in 1932 were known as Hoovervilles. In 1947 the mammoth Hoover Dam stretching 726 feet on the Colorado River was re-named in Hoover's honor. It had actually been completed in 1936.

Hoover died in 1964, just two years after posing at the library dedication with President Truman.

President Hoover, the first president to be born in Iowa and the first president to be born west of the Mississippi, was buried at the Herbert Hoover National Historic Site in West Branch, Iowa.

Presidential Sites:
Herbert Hoover Presidential Library, West Branch, Iowa, 319-643-5301
Herbert Hoover National Historic Site, West Branch, Iowa, 319-643-5301

Herbert Hoover

Getting Down to Business.
Editorial cartoon, 1932. $5-6

Don't Disturb the Water. Editorial
cartoon. 1932. $5-6

Hoover Wins 407 to 69.
New York Times newspaper,
1928. $40

Literary Digest.
October 1, 1932. $22

Hoover Mrs. Hoover. Real photo postcard. $2-3

President and Mrs. Hoover. Herbert Hoover
Presidential Library postcard. $5-6

President Herbert Hoover. Herbert Hoover Presidential Library postcard. $4-5

Home of Hoover in Palo Alto, California, Piltz Co. postcard. $2-3

Presidents Truman and Hoover. Herbert Hoover Presidential Library postcard. $6-8

Hoover Library and Museum. Dunlap-Henline Co. postcard. $1-2

State of Iowa. Real photo postcard. $2-3

Herbert Hoover

Birthplace in West Branch,
Iowa. Postcard. $2-3

Interior of Hoover birthplace.
Real photo postcard. $2-3

Herbert Hoover National
Historic Site. Official postcard
(modern)

Herbert Hoover Presidential Library.
Hoover Presidential Library postcard.
$2-3

Gravesite. Hoover National Historic Site. Official
postcard (modern)

Franklin D. Roosevelt

President 1933 - 1945

Although President Franklin D. Roosevelt was physically disabled, he became one of the most traveled presidents ever. It remains one of the major ironies of American presidential history.

Roosevelt, paralyzed by polio, was unable to walk. During the World War II years of his presidency he maneuvered himself with a cane and braces, or with the assistance of others. Still he traveled more than any president prior to that time, visiting leaders throughout the world.

Franklin Delano Roosevelt was born in 1882 at Hyde Park, New York. With a background of wealth and success of as a lawyer, FDR married Eleanor Roosevelt, the niece of President Theodore Roosevelt.

Even though disabled and often confined to a wheel chair, FDR became a skilled politician and went on to become elected as governor of New York both in 1928 and 1930.

The ever-popular Roosevelt was nominated as a candidate for president on the fourth ballot of the Democratic National Convention in 1932. He became the first presidential nominee to fly by airplane to the site of a national convention. FDR also became the first presidential nominee to make a personal speech of acceptance at a national convention.

Roosevelt campaigned on the New Deal theme that year, complete with a campaign song which promised, "Happy Days Are Here Again." He handily defeated Republican incumbent Herbert Hoover capturing 22 million votes and the electoral votes in all but six states. The victory made him only the third Democrat since the Civil War to be elected to the White House.

Early in 1933 Congress enacted the so-called New Deal legislation which basically dealt with recovery measures dealing with the economic woes of the Great Depression. That same year saw the creation of the National Recovery Administration and the Public Works Administration.

In one memorable postcard President Roosevelt is depicted behind the wheel "of his especially-equipped automobile" at the "Little White House" in Warm Springs, Georgia. It was a rare, however faint, in print reference to his disability. In effect the car had manual controls instead of foot pedals. The automobile bore 1935 license plates.

Decades later FDR's personal photographer Ollie Atkins wrote in the Saturday Evening Post of how clouded in secrecy the president's disability remained.

Noted Atkins:

"Everything done in those early years to conceal his infirmity. Today the public would know about such a thing. But then it was not generally realized that he had to be carried everywhere he went. And when we photographers finally got a chance to shoot him, it was all stage set in advance.

"He would be propped up in his chair at his desk, and it often looked as though his back was propped up as well. But FDR had that great smile and a fine head and somehow or other the pictures came off."

FDR defeated Republican opponent Alfred Landon to win re-election in 1936. He was re-elected again in 1940 on his way to becoming the first and only president to be elected to four terms.

Early in 1941 the Roosevelt Library and Museum was opened in Hyde Park, New York. The building, designed by President Roosevelt himself, was said to be characteristic of Dutch farmhouses in the Hudson Valley. It was the source of many postcards which often noted the museum and accompanying exhibit were open to the public, "Tuesday to Saturday, also Sundays and Holidays."

On December 7, 1941 the military of Japan attacked Guam, the Philippines, and Pearl Harbor in Hawaii igniting the flames of World War II. FDR's 'Day of Infamy' speech to the nation the follow day is still considered a milestone in the nation's history. President Roosevelt would not live to see the end of this great conflict.

As president Roosevelt often availed himself of physical therapy facilities in Warm Springs, Georgia. For most of the time however the grim years of the war exacted a heavy toll in FDR's health. Gray and grainy newsreel films frequently showed the president gaunt-faced and grimly aging almost week to week.

The 32nd president died suddenly at Warm Springs on April 12, 1945.

Presidential Sites:
Franklin D. Roosevelt Library & Museum, Hyde Park, New York, 914-229-8114
Little White House Historic Site, Warm Springs, Georgia, 706-655-5870
Roosevelt Campobello, Lubec, Maine, 506-752-2922

Roosevelt Winner In Landslide, *New York Times*, 1932. $40

Roosevelt Is Elected President, *Los Angeles Times*, 1932. $40

Franklin Delano Roosevelt, B-H Publication postcard. Ca. 1950s. $5-7

President Roosevelt at Little White House in Warm Springs, Georgia. Ca. 1940s. $5-6

A Study in Contrasts. Editorial cartoon, 1935. $5-6

The Political Medicine Show, Editorial cartoon, 1938. $3-4

President Roosevelt, Postcard from 1944 photograph.
Roosevelt Presidential Library and Museum postcard.

Franklin Roosevelt. Postcard based on 1945 painting
by Douglas Chandor. Smithsonian Institution

Franklin Roosevelt. Drawn image poster. 1930s. $50

President Roosevelt. Postcard based on unfinished
painting by Elizabeth Shoumatoff. Warm Springs
Memorial Commission postcard

Franklin D. Roosevelt

FRANKLIN AND ELEANOR ROOSEVELT

Franklin and
Eleanor Roosevelt.
Presidential Library
and Museum
Postcard. $4-5

Franklin D. Roosevelt. Little Debbie
premium card.1993. $1-2

Franklin Roosevelt. Campaign
chalkware wall plaque. $100

Roosevelt Dead. *Los Angeles
Times*, 1945. $30

Walk of States Stones.
Postcard from Little White
House at Warm Springs,
Georgia. $2-3

Roosevelt summer
home at Campobello
Island, New
Brunswick, Canada.
Ca. 1950s. Postcard.
$3-4

Sculpture based on
1933 photograph.
Franklin and Eleanor
Roosevelt. Roosevelt
Presidential Library
and Museum
Postcard

Roosevelt Presidential Library. Located in Hyde Park, New
York. Roosevelt Presidential Library and Museum Postcard

Statue of F.D.R. Postcard view of Grand Coulee Dam. Ca.
1950s. $3-4

Franklin D. Roosevelt

Harry S. Truman

President 1945 - 1953

President Harry S. Truman is credited with making the lone decision to usher in the era of the Atomic Bomb to the world.

On President Truman's orders two atomic bombs were dropped on Japanese cities in 1945. Those individual atomic explosions killed thousands of civilians and were responsible for ending World War II.

The person who would make such an awesome and historic decision was a person of humble, middle-America origins.

Harry Truman was born May 8, 1884 in Lamar, Missouri. He was the oldest of three children who were all raised on the family farm near Independence, Missouri. Truman's father was a farmer and a livestock dealer.

The family lived modestly, and the farm was mostly successful. Aside from a brief job as bank teller, Truman attended the family farm until age 33. He would eventually be the first president since U.S. Grant to have actually depended on farming for a living.

During World War I Truman joined the Missouri National Guard and served in France. His military career was impressive enough for him to earn a series of promotions from first lieutenant, to captain, and later to major.

The future 33rd president of the United States returned to Missouri after the war and married his childhood sweetheart Elizabeth Virginia "Bess" Wallace. The two attended school together since the fifth grade. They wed in 1919.

After a failed attempt at the retail business, Truman was elected to a county judgeship in 1922. Truman's daughter Mary Margaret was born in 1924. He generally held the office of judge until 1934 when he ran for United States Senator from the state of Missouri.

Truman was elected that year, and six years later he was elected by Missouri voters again. Truman's career in the senate was pretty much unremarkable aside from the Senate's Special Committee to Investigate the National Defense. It was said to have saved taxpayers grand sums of money.

Reports vary of how Truman became President Franklin Roosevelt's candidate for vice-president in 1944. Some say Roosevelt was simply unhappy with then vice-president Henry Wallace. Other accounts suggest at least four candidates were under serious consideration including Truman and that a major labor union leader favored Truman when asked by Roosevelt.

At any rate in the midst of World War II Truman found himself in the second ranking job in America.

Truman himself would later state that he had little contact with President Roosevelt and consequently no knowledge of top security matters including the so-called Atomic bomb.

Barely three months later Truman was summoned to the White House on a spring afternoon in April. He learned from Mrs. Roosevelt that President Roosevelt had died from a cerebral hemorrhage while in Warm Springs, Georgia. Shortly after 7 p.m. Truman was sworn in as the new president of the United States.

For the person from small town America it was a shocker.

"I felt the moon, the stars, and all the planets had fallen on me," he would later tell reporters. "I've got the most terribly responsible job a man ever had."

World War II continued its grim toll for another year. In May of 1945 Germany surrendered unconditionally to Allied Forces. The war with Japan meanwhile continued. By early August the decision by President Truman to drop the first atomic bomb on Japan was in full effect. On August 6 the first bomb struck Hiroshima killing thousands. Three days later a second atomic bomb was dropped, this time striking Nagasaki. Thousands more were killed.

"It was my fate to make the decision to use the first atomic bomb to bring about the end of a terrible war," he wrote in his book *Mr. Citizen* many years later. "Let us not be so preoccupied with weapons that we lose sight of the fact that war itself is the real villain and the scourge of mankind."

On September 2, 1945 less than a month after the bombings, the Japanese surrendered and signed terms aboard the U.S.S. Missouri.

Truman enjoyed some national popularity with the Truman Doctrine to aide Greece and Turkey in the 1947 cold war against communism. It was a tepid relationship by 1948 when he was nominated by the Democrat Party. By early fall Truman was well behind in most nationwide polls.

However despite his waning popularity Truman made a feisty campaigner. He toured the country for 35 days by train, making hundreds of whistle-stop visits to cheering crowds. He covered more than 30,000 miles by rail in what was later called the "Give 'em Hell" campaign. Rather than criticize his opponent Thomas Dewey directly, he blasted Congress instead. Later he would say his speeches were simply the truth which sounded "like hell" to members of Congress.

Truman pulled off a surprising election victory that year. One of the biggest goofs of that election was the Chicago Tribune's banner headline declaring, "Dewey Defeats Truman" on the evening the voting ended. A photograph of Truman holding a copy of that historic newspaper error became famous as well.

The White House itself was extensively renovated during the Truman years. While the Truman family lived in the nearby Blair House, nearly $6 million dollars worth of construction and repairs were undertaken at the official residence.

When North Korean forces crossed the 38th parallel and invaded the Republic of South Korea in June of 1950, President Truman ordered U.S. troops to the scene. General Douglas MacArthur led American forces who soon encountered Chinese Communist forces and the Korean War was fully ensued.

Eventually Truman and MacArthur had a falling out, and as a consequence the general was dismissed of command and ordered to return home in 1951.

Truman himself retired back to Independence in 1953. Even then he remained active in political affairs, and directed the establishment of the Harry S. Truman Library. Additionally he wrote three books of his memoirs including Mr. Citizen.

Presidential Sites:
Harry S. Truman Presidential Museum& Library, Independence, Missouri, 816-833-1400
Harry S. Truman National Historic Site, Independence, Missouri, 816-833-1400

HST A Pictorial Biography, Grosset & Dunlap, Inc. 1973. $6-7

Truman and Newspaper Error. Famous photograph of President Truman and mistaken 1948 newspaper headline in *The Chicago Tribune*, "Dewey Defeats Truman."
The original silver print of the Frank Cancellare photograph sold for $1,500 at Swann Galleries in 1992.

Harry S. Truman

Truman Leads Dewey.
New York Times, 1948.
$30

Mr. Citizen by
Harry Truman,
Published by
Bernard Geis
Associates,
1960. $7-8

Truman's Victory
Grows. *Los Angeles
Times*, 1948. $30

President Truman. Signed
photograph. *Courtesy of Skinner
Inc.* $275

The New Boss. Pathfinder
magazine, 1950. $3-4

President Harry Truman. Real photo
postcard. $8-10

President Truman and President Johnson Visit at the Truman Library. United Press International news photo. $8-10

Harry Truman Library and Museum at Independence, Mo. Postcard of Truman's 1941 Chrysler Royal coupe. $3-4

Home of President Truman. Inauguration Day Scene postcard. $4-5

Truman 33rd President, Is Dead. *New York Times*, 1972. $20

Harry S. Truman. Little Debbie premium card, 1993. $1-3

Truman Library and Museum. Postcard depicts reproduction of President Truman's office. $2-3

Dwight D. Eisenhower

President 1953 - 1961

During the middle of the 20th century and entire nation loved 'Ike', a decorated general who became president of the United States.

Dwight David Eisenhower, known to millions in the 1940s and 1950s as simply Ike, was the first president to preside over 50 states. At the time Ike was also the oldest president to ever serve in the White House.

Eisenhower was born October 14 of 1890 in Denison, Texas. Ultimately he would become the first president born in Texas. For the record however the Eisenhower family moved to Abilene, Kansas when Ike was very young. He spent his childhood there and attended public school there.

Historians could later also note that Eisenhower would become the last American president to be born in the 19th century.

Graduating from West Point Military Academy in 1915, Eisenhower was soon returning to his native state of Texas. Serving in a military post there he met and married Mamie Geneva Doud the following year.

After a long and distinguished military career General Dwight Eisenhower ended up as the Supreme Commander of Allied troops invading France on D-Day in 1944. Later a historical footnote would add that Ike was the only president to have served in uniform in both world wars.

Following WW II Eisenhower briefly became president of Columbia University before again returning to the military as Supreme Commander of NATO forces in1951. The following summer Eisenhower was nominated for president by the Republican National Convention in Chicago. A week later he resigned as General of the U.S. Army.

During that remarkable presidential campaign of 1952, the former general was re-introduced as Ike. The name was already familiar to those that followed the news during the grim days of the war, this time however it was a campaign slogan, "I Like Ike." Moreover it was the title of a campaign song written by the legendary Irving Berlin.

Ike and his running mate Richard Nixon waged a highly successful campaign against Democrat nominee Adlai Stevenson and his vice-presidential nominee John Sparkman. When it was over Ike had won handily capturing more than 33 million votes nationwide. In 1953, the same year he was sworn into office, Eisenhower directed the signing of a truce in the Korean War.

In 1955 Eisenhower conducted the first presidential news conference to be recorded both by newsreels and television cameras. The event was not "live" but instead was held until official release by the White House. That same year he suffered a heart attack while on vacation in Colorado. He remained hospitalized for seven weeks.

Ike won re-election in 1956, this time gathering more than 35 million votes and more than 86 percent of the electoral votes. Following the victory Ike and Mamie found time to spend a few days in their 'new' home in Gettysburg, Pennsylvania. Ironically the famed brick farmhouse on the edge of Gettysburg National Military Park was the only home they ever owned together.

In a *Country Gentleman* magazine article of that era, Ike described how it happened:

> "The house, dwarfed by an immense barn, was located at the end of a private dirt lane a half mile long. Mamie had found the place she wanted."

Uniquely in 1959 both Hawaii and Alaska became states of the union, and President Eisenhower became the first president to hold office for 50 states.

After serving as the nation's 34th president, Ike left the White House in January of 1961. Then at age 70 he was the oldest person to hold the high office. Ironically he was succeeded by John F. Kennedy, then the youngest person to ever hold the office.

Ike lived the rest of his years back on the farm at Gettysburg. He died in March of 1969 after an extended illness. His body was carried by train across the United States before he was buried near his childhood home in Abilene, Kansas.

The inscription on his tombstone reads:

> "A great man passed this way in defense of freedom."

Presidential Sites:

Dwight D. Eisenhower Library & Museum, Abilene, Kansas, 785-263-4751

Eisenhower National Historic Site, Gettysburg, Pennsylvania, 717-338-9114

Right:
Dwight David Eisenhower.
1950s-era postcard. $5-6

Eisenhower By A Landslide. *Los Angeles Times* newspaper, 1952. $22

USA. Postcard reproduction of poster. $3-4

President Dwight Eisenhower. News photo of 1966 portrait. United Press International. $5-6

General Eisenhower. Postcard of portrait by Thomas Stephens. $3-4

The President of the U.S. *Time* magazine, July 4, 1955. $3-5

Eisenhower Says He Will Seek 2nd Term. *New York Times* newspaper, 1956. $22

Dwight D. Eisenhower

General of the Army. 1950s era postcard. $4-5

Eisenhower Home. Real photo postcard. $3-4

Eisenhower Home, 1898-1946. 1960s-era postcard. $2-3

Eisenhower Presidential Library. Posted 1963. $2-3

Home in Gettysburg, Pa. 1950s era postcard. $2-3

Eisenhower center at Abilene, Kansas. 1960s-era postcard. $2-3

John F. Kennedy

President 1961 - 1963

John F. Kennedy, at age 43, was the youngest president to enter the White House. Kennedy was the first American president to have been born in the 20th century.

He was also the first person of the Catholic faith to be elected President of the United States.

The man who would be the 35th president was born May 29, 1917 in a suburb of Boston, Brookline, Massachusetts. He was educated in private schools and then Harvard University, where he graduated with honors.

With the outbreak of World War II, Kennedy enlisted in the U.S. Navy and was commissioned a lieutenant. In 1943 Kennedy's PT boat was rammed by a Japanese Destroyer in the Solomon Islands. Kennedy suffered a serious back injury but was able to lead survivors to the sanctuary of a small island.

Out of the military in 1946 Kennedy entered the Democratic primary as a congressional candidate in a district near Boston. He won the primary handily and was also victorious in the general election. At age 28 he was a Member of Congress.

In 1952 he was elected U.S. Senator from the state of Massachusetts, and the following year he married the lovely Jacqueline Bouvier. In 1955 while recovering from back surgery he wrote the book *Profiles in Courage* which in turn won the Pulitzer Prize in history.

Kennedy narrowly lost the nomination for vice president in 1956 during a relatively dramatic Democrat Party national convention. Four years later after a success in a series of primaries he was nominated for president on the first ballot of his party's convention.

Television debates were a major factor in that 1960 presidential race between Kennedy and Republican contender Richard Nixon. The two candidates were the first two in history to debate nationwide on the medium of television. Kennedy won the electoral vote that year 303 to 219, but the popular vote was decided by little more than 100,000 votes.

In his inaugural address Kennedy urged Americans to "ask not what your country can do for you. Ask what you can do for your country." He also spoke of "the struggle against the common enemies of man: tyranny, poverty and war itself."

Early on, in April of 1961, the Kennedy administration blundered by attempting an invasion of Cuba with Cuban exiles attempting to overthrow the regime of Fidel Castro. The mission failed to establish a beachhead at a place known as the Bay of Pigs.

The Kennedy administration was more successful with Cuban Missile Crisis the following year. In October of 1962 air reconnaissance discovered that leaders of the Soviet Union were attempting to install nuclear missiles. Kennedy ordered a quarantine on all weapons bound for Cuba, and ultimately 13 days later the Soviets agreed to withdraw the missiles.

A plaque on Kennedy's oval office desk bore this inscription:

"Oh God, thy sea is so great and my boat so small."

During his three years in the White House President Kennedy did make progress on the space program, Civil Rights, and the Peace Corps. Six weeks before his death he also completed the Test Ban Treaty halting nuclear testing in earth's atmosphere. The treaty was signed by the Soviet Union, Great Britain, and the United States.

Just slightly more than 1,000 days after entering the White House, President Kennedy was killed by an assassin's rifle as Kennedy's motorcade wound through Dallas, Texas.

Events relating to the death of President Kennedy remain controversial. Lee Harvey Oswald was arrested in connection with the assassination but was shot and killed before he could be brought to trial. Decades later some experts and historians disagree on details of this grim episode.

In addition to being the youngest president to enter office, he was also the youngest president to die in office.

Presidential Sites:

John F. Kennedy Library, Boston, Massachusetts, 617-514-1600

John Fitzgerald Kennedy National Historic Site, Brookline, Massachusetts, 617-566-7937

Kennedy's Summer Home on Cap Cod. E.D. West Co. postcard. $3-4

Kennedy and Nixon in 1960 election. Decision trading card, 1993. $1-3

Kennedy and Eisenhower. Decision trading card. 1992. $1-3

Kennedy Nearing Victory. *Los Angeles Times* newspaper, 1960. $10-12

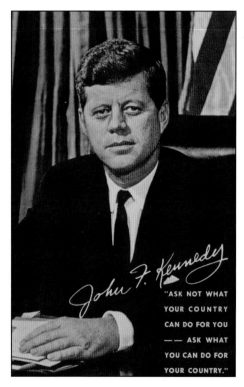

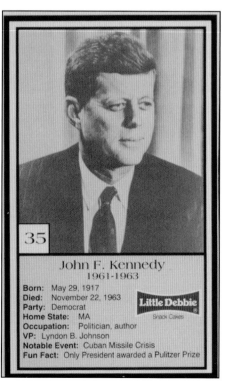

John F. Kennedy. In Memoriam postcard. $3-4

Presidents of the Untied States. 1960s-era postcard. $2-3

John F. Kennedy. Little Debbie premium card. 1993. $2-3

John F. Kennedy. Colonial Bread
premium card. 1976. $1-3

Caroline and JFK. United Press
International photo. 1963. $30.

The Kennedys. Official 1960 campaign
photograph. $30-40

Kennedy Is Killed
By Sniper. *New York
Times*, 1963. $20

President
Kennedy's
Summer
Home.
Lockwood
Studios
postcard.
$3-4

Assassination Scene.
1960s-era postcard.
$2-3

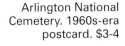

Arlington National
Cemetery. 1960s-era
postcard. $3-4

Lyndon B. Johnson

President 1963 - 1969

Lyndon Baines Johnson became president of the United States upon the assassination of President John F. Kennedy in November of 1963. On that tragic day LBJ became the first and only president to take the oath of office aboard an airplane.

It was given little note at the time, but Johnson was the first president to be given the oath of office by a woman. The woman was Federal Judge Sarah Hughes. Also in the gender category LBJ was the first president to take the oath with his wife holding the Bible.

Ironically Johnson was the first American president in history to be present at the actual assassination of the person he would replace in office.

Johnson was born August 27, 1908 near Stonewall, Texas. Decades later the LBJ birthplace would be declared a national historical park. At the time it was the only presidential home to receive such official status.

Years later LBJ would graduate from Southwest Texas State and become a school teacher. In 1930 he taught English at Sam Houston High School, later he became a teacher and principal at a Mexican-American school in Cotulla, Texas.

Lyndon married Claudia Alta Johnson in 1934. His bride had been nicknamed Lady Bird by her family's maid when she was only two years old. The Lady Bird name stayed with her throughout her entire life.

In 1937 Johnson turned to politics and won a special election to fill the Congressional seat of a U.S. representative who had died in office. The following year LBJ won the general election and eventually served several terms before being elected United States Senator in 1948.

When the 1960 presidential election year rolled around Johnson was again a candidate for the U.S. Senate, but he also had loftier political ambitions. That summer he was nominated for president at the Democrat National Convention. He garnered more than 400 votes but lost to John Kennedy. A short time later JFK surprised many by selecting Johnson as his running mate.

In the general election the Kennedy-Johnson ticket narrowly defeated Republicans Richard Nixon and Henry Cabot Lodge to claim the White House. Interestingly Johnson had also been re-elected as U.S. Senator. He resigned his third term as senator just minutes after being sworn in as vice-president of the United States.

Johnson's political office changed quite dramatically again three years later when JFK was shot and killed as both men rode in a parade in Dallas, Texas. By a dark coincidence, LBJ became the second vice-president named Johnson to replace an assassination. The same thing had transpired nearly a century earlier when Abraham Lincoln was killed and Andrew Johnson succeeded to the office of president.

Near the end of that eventful day Johnson and a small group of others gathered on Air Force One as it sat on Love Field. After a brief ceremony President Johnson issued his very first order as commander-in-chief, "Let's get airborne."

Just days later Johnson appointed a seven-person commission head by Supreme Court justice Earl Warren to investigate the terrible assassination of President Kennedy. It was known forever more simply as the Warren Commission.

During his presidential years Johnson was a major force in passing and signing civil rights, anti-poverty, and tax reduction legislation. He also established the Texas White House at his ranch home near Johnson City, Texas. Lady Bird meanwhile was instrumental in the promotion of highway and civic beautification.

In 1964 Johnson launched his own presidential bid with the catchy slogan, "All The Way With LBJ." In the midst of that campaign the Saturday Evening Post commented on the nature of the campaign and the candidate:

"The man the crowds will remember is the earthy Texan, campaigning in the streets like any crossroads candidate for Congress, kissing small children, reaching out scratched and swollen hands to any hand that reaches out to him, rasping hoarsely through a bullhorn from the backseat of an open car."

That year LBJ won easily with 61 percent of the national vote, the greatest percentage of any president in history at the time. Johnson himself wrote of the path before him:

"The challenge of the next half century is whether we have the wisdom to use our wealth to enrich and elevate our national life, and to advance the quality of American civilization."

Despite many achievements, the nation's division and disenchantment over the war in Vietnam forced LBJ to decline a second presidential term in 1968.

The 36th president of the United States, died on January 22, 1974 in San Antonio, Texas.

Presidential Sites:
Lyndon Baines Johnson Library, Austin, Texas, 512-482-5137
Lyndon Baines Johnson National Historical Park, Johnson City, Texas, 512-868-7128

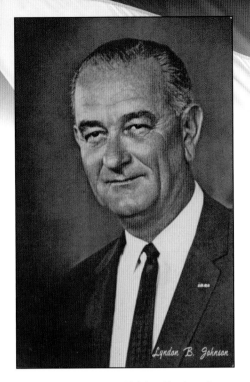

Lyndon B. Johnson, Fabian Bachrach
postcard. $5-6

The 36th President. Postcard of painting
by Elizabeth Shoumatoff. $3-4

President Lyndon Johnson, 1960s-era
postcard. $3-4

Johnson Swamps
Goldwater. *New York
Times*, 1964. $20

Lyndon Banes
Johnson. Colonial
Bread premium
card. 1976. $1-3

Presidents
of the United
States.
1960s-era
postcard.
$1-2

Who Won—
And Why.
Newsweek,
Nov 9, 1964.
$5

L B J Ranch Home - "The Texas White House"

Lyndon B. Johnson   Roger D. Branigin

Entrance to the L B J Ranch

Left, from top;
Birthplace in Stonewall, Texas. Johnson National Historical Site postcard. $2-3

L. B. J. Ranch Home. Burrell-Ford Co. postcard. $2-3

Texas White House at Johnson City, Texas. Davis Merchandise postcard. $2-3

President Johnson Birthplace. Armstrongs' Western postcard. $1-3

Above, from top;
Eldon Tipton and President Johnson. Dated August 6, 1964. $2-3

1964 campaign postcard. President Johnson and Indiana Governor Roger Branigin. $3-4

Entrance to L.B.J. Ranch. Nowonty-Burrell Co. postcard. $1-3

Richard M. Nixon

President 1969 - 1974

Richard Milhous Nixon was the first American president to visit all 50 states. He was the first president to visit China, and the first to ever resign.

Nixon was born in Yorba Linda a suburb of Los Angeles in 1913. He grew up in a working class Quaker family, and as youngster worked in the family grocery store.

A good student he earned high grades at Whittier College. Nixon also met his future wife Thelma Catherine "Pat" Ryan when both had roles in an amateur production play there. After Whittier College he moved on to Duke University Law School where he graduated with honors.

Richard and Pat were married in 1940. Eventually they would have two children, Patricia "Tricia" and Julie.

The future president interrupted his brief law practice to serve in the Navy as a lieutenant commander during World War II.

Out of the military and back in civilian life, Nixon became a candidate for Congress in 1946. He won and was off to Washington.

As a congressman Nixon gained national attention fighting Communist influences as a member of the House Un-American Activities Committee. That attention no doubt was one of the factors that propelled Nixon on to the national presidential ticket in 1952 with Republican nominee Dwight "Ike" Eisenhower. Just two years earlier Nixon had been elected U.S. Senator from California.

The two made a successful team and at age 39 Nixon was elected Vice President of the United States. Four years later they repeated the national victory.

In 1960 Nixon won the Republican Party's presidential nomination by acclamation. Nixon lost his bid for the presidency that year to Democrat John F. Kennedy. Experts blamed the loss in part to Nixon's lackluster showing in a series of nationally televised debates with Kennedy.

Two years later Richard Nixon campaigned to become governor of California. He lost that election and generally put politics aside for a career with a New York law firm.

Back in the thick of political things in 1968 Nixon won the Republican presidential nomination and went on to capture 55 percent of the Electoral College in the general election. He essentially defeated two candidates that year, Democrat Hubert Humphrey and third-party candidate George Wallace.

In the White House the Nixon administration pushed revenue sharing and an end to the draft. It was also during the Nixon years that Americans made the first moon landing.

Nixon made history in 1972 with a journey to China and Russia. As the first American president to visit China he met with Chairman Mao Tse-tung. Later he met with leaders of the Soviet Union and signed the first SALT Treaty (Strategic Arms Limitations Treaty)

President Nixon ran for re-election as president in 1972. He defeated Democrat George McGovern by a wide margin. Four years earlier he had won 55 percent of the Electoral College vote; in 1972 he garnered 96 percent of the electoral vote.

However, serious problems for the Nixon administration began even before the presidential campaign had ended. Police arrested five men who had burglarized the headquarters of the National Democratic Committee in the Watergate building in Washington, D.C. The suspects were apparently installing wiretapping devices.

Within a few months the Nixon administration was embattled over the growing "Watergate" scandal. Eventually the break-in was traced to officials of the Committee to Re-elect the President. As a result a number of administration officials resigned, and some were convicted of crimes connected with efforts to cover up the affair. While Nixon repeatedly denied any personal involvement, tape recordings ordered released by the courts indicated otherwise.

Faced with almost certain impeachment, Nixon announced on August 8, 1974 that he would resign the next day to begin, "that process of healing which is so desperately needed in America."

Afterwards Nixon flew home to San Clemente, California. In September of 1974 President Gerald Ford granted Nixon a full pardon.

"Each moment in history is a fleeting time, precious and unique," said President Nixon in his inaugural address of 1969. "But some stand out as moments of beginning, in which courses are set that shape decades or centuries."

Presidential Site:
Richard Nixon Library and Birthplace, Yorba Linda, California, 714-993-3393

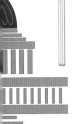

Nixon Edging Close To Magic 270. *Los Angeles Times* newspaper, 1968. $20

Landslide Victory For Nixon. *Los Angeles Times*, 1972. $15

First Monday magazine. November 6, 1973. $6-8

President Richard Nixon. Inaugural photo postcard. $5-6

Pat Nixon and Tricia Nixon Cox. Resignation scene postcard. $3-4

Nixon in Knoxville, Tennessee. United Press International photo. 1968. $20.

President Nixon in Franklin, Indiana. News photograph. 1971. $4-5

Spiro Agnew and Richard Nixon. United Press International news photograph. 1968. $25

Left, from top;
Nixon and Premier Hua Guofeng. Postcard of Ex-president Nixon in China. 1976. $3-4

Apollo 11 Moon Landing. Postcard dated July 20, 1969. $5-6

Birthplace in Yorba Linda, California. Columbia postcard. $2-3

Inn in San Clemente, California. Amescolor postcard. $2-3

Above, from top;
Nixon Visits China. Postcard of Ex-president and Mrs. Nixon in Peking, 1976. $3-4

Nixon Resigns. Resignation scene postcard. $3-4

President Nixon and Mrs. Nixon. 1969 postcard. $4-5

Richard M. Nixon

Gerald Ford

President 1974 - 1977

President Gerald Ford was remembered for many presidential-related firsts in his career including the first president ever to take oath during the month August.

Ford was the first Vice President selected under the terms of the Twenty Fifth Amendment to the United States constitution. That dramatic event occurred in 1973 upon the resignation of Vice President Spiro Agnew.

Just one year later, in 1974, in the aftermath of the Watergate scandal President Richard Nixon resigned. Thus Ford became the first president in history to assume the high office based on a presidential resignation.

Then perhaps the most historic first, President Ford became the first president in American history to have held both White House offices without a single vote from the public citizenry.

While Ford served a relatively brief term in the White House, postcards also recorded his tenure there. Postcards also documented his political life prior to that time, the Ford Presidential Library, and other occurrences.

Ford, whose Secret Service code name was Pass Key, had still another first in connection with the presidency. He was the first president to be born from the state of Nebraska. The man who would be president was born on July 14, 1913 in Omaha, Nebraska.

After graduating from high school in Grand Rapids, Michigan he attended and graduated from the University of Michigan in 1935. Later he graduated from Yale Law School in 1941 just in time to serve in the military at the onset of World War II. During the war he attained the rank of lieutenant commander in the U.S. Navy.

Following the war he returned to Grand Rapids where he opened a law practice.

Two major events occurred just a few weeks apart in 1948. First he married Elizabeth Bloomer, and second he was elected to the U.S. Congress.

After a distinguished career in Congress, Ford was eventually elected House minority leader. When scandal forced Nixon's vice president to resign from office in 1973, Ford was chosen as a replacement. The formality became an historical one because it represented the first enactment of the 25th Amendment. Under its stipulation the president was permitted to appoint a replacement vice president with the approval of Congress once the office became vacant for any reason.

As events would unfold Ford scarcely had time to adjust to the new job. The following year Nixon himself resigned moving Ford to the highest office in the land without a single citizen ballot.

"Ford was confronted with almost insuperable tasks," notes the official White House website. "There were the challenges of mastering inflation, reviving a depressed economy, solving chronic energy shortages, and trying to ensure world peace."

There was also the matter of the Nixon pardon. Granting the ex-president a full pardon for any federal crimes he might have committed while in office created a public furor and for a time curtailed his national popularity.

Throughout his term Ford publicly considered himself to be "a moderate in domestic affairs, a conservative in fiscal affairs, and a dyed-in-the-wool internationalist in foreign affairs." According to the official White House site a major Ford presidency goal was to help businesses operate more freely by reducing taxes upon it and easing the controls exercised by regulatory agencies. He was quoted as saying, "we ... declared our independence 200 years ago, and we are not about to lose it now to paper shufflers and computers."

President Ford survived two assassination attempts in 1975, both in the same month of September.

Ford won a battle for the Republican nomination for what would have been his first truly elected term as president in 1976. He lost in November however to his opponent former Governor Jimmy Carter of Georgia.

Somewhat ironically it was President Carter who paid tribute to President Ford during his Inauguration Day speech. "For myself and for our Nation," Carter said, "I want to thank my predecessor for all he has done to heal our land."

President Gerald Ford, whose favorite ice cream was said to be butter pecan, died peacefully at his home in Rancho, California in late December of 2006. He was 93 years of age.

Presidential Sites:

Gerald R. Ford Library, Ann Arbor, Michigan, 313-741-2218

Gerald R. Ford Museum, Grand Rapids, Michigan, 616-451-9263

A Question of Values. *First Monday* magazine, 1976. $8

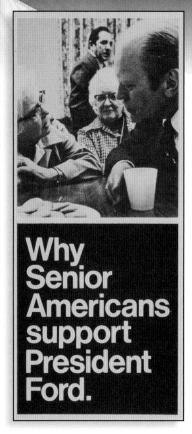

Why Senior Americans Support Ford. Campaign brochure, 1976. $2-3

President Gerald Ford. Postcard of official presidential photograph. Gerald Ford Presidential Museum postcard

Ford Wins Nomination. GOP convention in Kansas City. Gerald Ford Presidential Museum postcard

Magazine illustration of the 1976 GOP National Convention.

President Ford Says "Nightmare Over." *Los Angeles Times* newspaper, 1974. $12

President Ford. Postcard of portrait by Everett Kinstler. Gerald R. Ford Museum postcard

President Ford at Carter inauguration. Coral-Lee postcard. $3-4

Vice President Ford. Real photo postcard. $2-3

President and Mrs. Ford. Postcard from 1992 photograph. Gerald R. Ford Museum postcard

Presidents and Guests. Postcard depicts 1981 dedication of Ford Presidential Museum. $5-6

Betty Ford. Coral-Lee postcard. $3-4

Jimmy Carter

President 1977 - 1981

Jimmy Carter always claimed to be just a country boy who became president. And he was just that.

Carter was born October 1, 1924 in a town so small it could lay claim to only two grocery stores, one hardware store, and about 500 citizens. The community was Plains, Georgia; and his father was a peanut farmer.

While his birth certificate read James Earl Carter Jr., he was simply known as Jimmy from childhood forward. As a young man he left the peanut farm for the United States Naval Academy in Annapolis, Maryland. He graduated in 1946 with honors, and would in fact eventually be the first president to have graduated from the Naval Academy.

Immediately after graduation he married Rosalynn Smith. Together they would have four children—John William (Jack), James Earl II (Chip), Donnel Jeffery (Jeff) and Amy Lynn. Carter served seven years as a naval officer and spent part of that time studying nuclear physics as part of the Navy's nuclear submarine program.

He resigned his commission as a senior-grade lieutenant when his father died in 1953 and returned to peanut farming. Back on the farm Carter expanded the operation to a full 1,500 acres and began purchasing peanuts from other growers as well. Additional warehouses and processing machinery were incorporated into the business.

Achieving a near half million dollar business venture, Carter turned in part to politics. In 1963 at age 38 he was elected a Georgia state senator. By 1970 he had launched a successful campaign to be governor of Georgia.

As governor he became a rising star among southern governors. He stressed efficiency in government and the environment, and the removal of racial barriers. It seemed to pay off.

In 1974 Governor Carter announced his candidacy for the Democratic Party nomination for president. Mostly by himself he began a two-year campaign that gradually gained traction around the country. At the Democrat National Convention he was nominated on the first ballot. He selected Senator Walter Mondale as his running mate.

Carter waged an energetic campaign and engaged incumbent Gerald Ford on three nationally televised debates. His campaign slogan was, Leadership for a Change. In November of 1976 Carter won the electoral vote 297 to 241. Thus Carter became the first governor to be elected president since Franklin Roosevelt, and the first president from the "Deep South" in the 20th century.

President Carter and First Lady Rosalynn walked in the 1977 inaugural parade, waving at the throngs of people along the streets. With them was their nine-year old daughter. In doing so, President Carter became the first president to walk the one and one half mile parade route from the Capitol to the White House during such an inaugural parade.

At the White House in 1978 Carter played a key role in bringing about a peace treaty between Israel and Egypt. Moreover Carter did establish a national energy policy, added 100 million acres in Alaska to the nation park system, and established the Department of Education.

However those successes were over-shadowed by the nation's eroding economy. By 1980 the rate of inflation was 80 percent and the price of gold had climbed to over $700 an ounce. Worse still, motorists at the gas pump were shocked to see gasoline go over $1 a gallon.

On the foreign scene things were just as grim. When the Soviet Union invaded Afghanistan the president reacted with a grain embargo and a boycott of the Moscow Olympic Games of 1980. Later Iranian students seized the U.S. Embassy in Iran and seized 52 American hostages. The Americans remained hostages as one year ticked into another. They were not released until the day President Carter left office and President Ronald Reagan took office.

Carter left the White House but continued humanitarian and diplomatic efforts in various parts of the world. He is a farmer, engineer, naval officer, business operator, governor, and also the 39th president of the United States.

Presidential Sites:

Jimmy Carter Library & Museum, Atlanta, Georgia, 404-331-3942

Jimmy Carter National Historic Site, Plains, Georgia, 229-824-4104

Jimmy Carter

Jimmy Carter. Postcard from official White House Photo. $3-4

Carter and German leader Helmut Schmidt. Coral-Lee postcard. $2-3

Carter Is Victor In Tight Race. *Los Angles Times*, 1976. $6

President Jimmy Carter. Coral-Lee Inaugural postcard. 1977. $3-4

Rosalynn and Jimmy Carter. Coral-Lee postcard. 1977. $2-3

President and Mrs. Carter. Inaugural postcard. $3-4

Vice President Mondale and President Carter. Coral-Lee Inaugural postcard. $2-3

Left, from top;
Jimmy Carter in England.
Coral-Lee postcard. 1977.
$2-3

Tour of Gettysburg
Battlefield. Coral-Lee
postcard. 1978. $2-3

Visiting A Steel Mill. Coral-
Lee postcard. $2-3

President Carter and
journalists. Official White
House photo. 1977. $4-5

Above, from top;
Presidential Ball. Coral-
Lee postcard. 1977. $2-3

President Carter and
Israeli Prime Minister
Begin. Coral-Lee
postcard. 1977. $2-3

Presidential Couples.
Coral-Lee White House
reception postcard. $2-3

Jimmy Carter

Ronald Reagan

President 1981 - 1989

Postcards were well past their heyday during the administration of President Ronald Reagan, yet they did catch the highlights of his presidency.

Ironically President Reagan was born early in 1911 near the height of the postcard's appeal and usage. Reagan was born in an apartment above the bank in downtown Tampico, Illinois. Later he lived in another Main Street apartment above the variety store in the same town.

Among his other accomplishments, Reagan was the first president to be born in the state of Illinois. He graduated from Eureka College in 1932 and became a sports announcer on radio.

Just five years later he had left the state and headed west to Hollywood. Probably his most famous role came in the film *Knute Rockne—All American* where he played legendary Notre Dame football player George Gipp. He made numerous other films however, including *King's Row, Santa Fe Trail, Storm Warning, Hellcats of the Navy,* and *Cattle Queen of Montana.* He also co-starred with a chimpanzee in 1951's *Bedtime for Bonzo.*

During the 1950s and into the early 1960s Reagan was host of television's General Electric Theatre. During that second decade he also hosted television's Death Valley Days sponsored by 20-Mule-Team Borax.

In the middle 1960s Reagan was encouraged to run for governor of California by fellow Republicans. The movie star turned politician challenged and defeated incumbent Governor Edmund "Pat" Brown. Four years later Governor Reagan was re-elected for a second term.

Reagan supporters skirmished with followers of President Gerald Ford at the 1976 Republican National Convention. Ford won the nomination but Reagan made a national impression. He handily won the GOP nomination in 1980.

Campaigning with the slogan "Let's Make America Great Again" he defeated incumbent President Jimmy Carter that year. Reagan garnered 489 electoral votes compared to 49 for President Carter. At age 69 on November 4 of 1980 Reagan became the oldest person to be elected President of the United States.

In March of 1981 Reagan was shot in an assassination attempt as he was leaving the Washington Hilton Hotel. The injury turned out to be much more serious than the public or even the President realized. He was rushed to George Washington University at first believing that the pain in his upper body was caused by rough treatment from the Secret Service. A trauma team removed a bullet from his chest. His recovery took nearly two months.

Four years after his first presidential election and now at age 73 President Reagan did even better in his re-election effort. In 1984 he captured 525 electoral votes and nearly 60 percent of the vote. The temperature for the first inaugural was a mild 56 degrees. On inauguration day in 1984 it was a chilling zero in Washington, D.C. The traditional parade was canceled for the first time ever, and ceremonies were held inside.

His years in the White House were richly recorded on postcards later published by Coral-Lee of Cordova, California. Among them were scenes of the President and First Lady Nancy Reagan in various locations ranging from Washington University Hospital to the White House. The postcards additionally depict Reagan with Egyptian President Anwar Sadat, and in a group at the North-South Summit at Cancun, Mexico.

One particular postcard in the series depicts Nancy Reagan with actor Gary Coleman on the set of the television comedy series Different Strokes.

Regarding his wife, Reagan was often quoted as saying, "She has been the most important influence on my life."

In 1994 the former president disclosed that he had Alzheimer's disease in the hope of increasing public awareness. He died of complications of that illness ten years later at age 93.

When he addressed the country for the last time President Reagan concluded:

"I now begin the journey that will lead me into the sunset of my life. I know for America there will always be a bright dawn ahead."

Presidential Site:
Ronald Reagan Presidential Library, Simi Valley, California, 800-410-8354

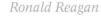

Ronald Reagan, 40th President.
Silberne Sales postcard. $5-6

Ronald Reagan Will Become
President. *Weekly Reader*,
1981. $6-8

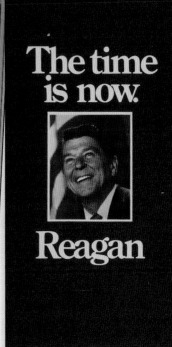

President
Ronald
Reagan.
Roberts
postcard. $6-8

The time is now. Reagan.
1980 campaign brochure. $5

The Honorable Ronald Reagan. Republican $100 A Plate
Dinner, 1975. $4-5

Reagan Takes Office. *The Los Angeles Times*, 1981. $8

Inaugural Escort badge. 1981 Reagan Inauguration. $5

Hospitalized after assassination attempt. Coral-Lee postcard. 1981. $3-4

Four presidents at Sadat funeral. Coral-Lee postcard. 1981. $4-5

The Reagans. Coral-Lee postcard. 1981. $3-4

Governor Reagan and President Carter. Coral-Lee postcard. 1981. $2-3

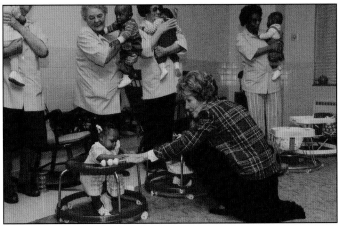

Left, from top;
President Reagan and Mrs. Reagan. R.W. Coffman postcard. $4-5

First Lady in Hyattsville, Maryland. Coral-Lee postcard. 1981. $2-3

President Reagan and Menachem Begin. Coral-Lee postcard. 1981. $2-3

Nancy Reagan in classroom. Coral-Lee postcard. 1982. $2-3

Above, from top;
President Reagan in Nevada. Governor List campaign postcard. $4-5

First Lady and Ron Jr. Coral-Lee postcard. 1981. $2-3

Reagan at North-South Summit. Coral-Lee postcard. 1981. $2-3

Ronald Reagan

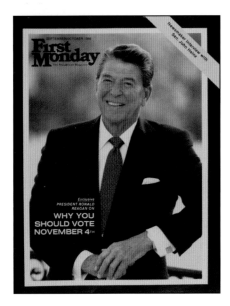

President Reagan. *First Monday* magazine, 1986. $4

First Lady and Lucky. Official White House photo. $35

President Reagan and Anwar Sadat. Coral-Lee postcard. 1981. $2-3

Reagan Again. 1984 campaign poster. $22

First couple greets flower girl. Coral-Lee postcard. 1982. $3-4

Nancy Reagan presents American Cancer Society awards. Coral-Lee postcard. 1982. $2-3

Nancy Reagan at Easter Event. Coral-Lee postcard. 1983. $2-3

Modern Presidents

Many years ago there was a joke about not fully trusting candidates seeking the office of president.

As the story goes Mary Lee was milking in the front yard of the family farm while her mother was busy at work in the kitchen.

Presently a car stops at the edge of the road and a person emerges from the vehicle. After a while the girl's curious mother calls to her daughter and asks whom she is talking to.

Mary Lee answers that she is talking to a person seeking to be president.

"Get inside here immediately," the woman shouts to the girl, "and bring the cow with you."

Perhaps in the past quarter century a waiting public has been less skeptical and more understanding of those seeking the office of the presidency as well of those who finally achieve it.

One thing for certain has been that so-called modern presidents have prevailed with relatively few postcards. There were some of course, as well as 'photo cards', mailers, and variations of all the above. But the standard postcard- for many reasons- ceased to be the White House method it once proudly was.

George H. W. Bush

President 1989 - 1993

George Herbert Walker Bush, considered a true war hero, was the last veteran of World War II to serve as President of the United States.

Bush was born June 12, 1924 in Milton, Massachusetts, to Senator Prescott Bush and Dorothy Walker Bush.

At age 18 Bush became the youngest naval aviator in American history. He joined the military service in 1941 shortly after enemy attacks on Pearl Harbor. During WW II he flew 58 combat missions. In one dramatic mission as a torpedo bomber pilot he was shot down by Japanese anti-aircraft gunfire. He was eventually rescued from hostile waters by an American submarine. Ultimately Bush was awarded the Distinguished Flying Cross for bravery.

Following the Second World War Bush attended Yale University. He married Barbara Pierce in January of 1945. Their marriage produced six children including John "Jeb" Bush who would eventually become governor of Florida and George Walker Bush who would eventually himself became President of the United States.

The senior Bush graduated from Yale in 1948. An enterprising Bush moved West after graduation and emerged in the oil business. By the time George Herbert Walker Bush was 40 years old he was a millionaire.

Soon after founding his own oil company Bush became involved in Republican Party politics. He served two terms in the United States House of Representatives. He ran unsuccessfully for the United States Senate twice before going on to serve in a number of national governmental and political roles.

At one time or another Bush was Ambassador to the Untied Nations, chairman of the Republican National Committee, Chief of the U.S. Liaison Office in the People's Republic of China, and director of the Central Intelligence Agency.

Bush stepped into the national political spotlight in 1980 as a candidate for President of the United States. He lost the Republican nomination to Ronald Reagan. Presidential nominee Reagan however selected Bush to be his running mate that year. When the two gained the White House then Vice President Bush was given significant responsibilities including areas of Federal deregulation and fighting drug abuse on a national scale.

After eight years in a partnership with President Reagan, Bush won the 1988 Republican nomination for president. At the same convention Bush selected Dan Quayle of Indiana as his running mate. That fall Bush easily defeated the Democratic presidential nominee Massachusetts Governor Michael Dukakis.

"We are a nation of communities," Bush told the nation, "…a brilliant diversity spread like stars, like a thousand points of light in a broad and peaceful sky."

On becoming the 41st President of the United States President Bush pledged at his inaugural, "a kinder and gentler nation…rich with promise."

While President Bush was in office the Berlin Wall came down, as did the overall structure of the once powerful Soviet Union. There were true military conflicts elsewhere however during the Bush term.

The president made a major but controversial decision in sending American troops into Panama to deal with the regime of General Manuel Noriega. As a result the Panama Canal was secured and Noriega was brought to trial in the United States on drug trafficking charges. Noriega was convicted of those charges and ultimately imprisoned.

Bigger trouble loomed for the Bush presidency when Iraqi forces under the command of Saddam Hussein invaded the neighboring country of Kuwait. After talks with the United Nations and Congress, President Bush dispatched 425,000 troops to the region. The U.N. and allied nations provided more than 100,000 additional troops. In the end the military campaign known as Desert Storm defeated Iraq's so-called million-man army and secured Kuwait.

Back at home the nation's economy was an issue in the 1992 election year. Although interest and inflation rates were relatively low the nation's midyear unemployment had reached 7.8 percent, the highest such figure in eight years. Despite the Bush administration's efforts to increase federal spending for education, childcare and technology research by the Census Bureau confirmed that 14.2 percent of the American population lived in poverty. Despite accomplishments such as the American Disabilities Act, there were growing concerns that year about the federal deficit and other economic issues.

In November of 1992 President Bush was defeated in his effort at re-election by Democrat William Jefferson Clinton.

Presidential Site:
George Bush Presidential Library & Museum, College Station, Texas, 409-260-9552

Bush is elected President.
Chicago Tribune, 1988.
$4-5

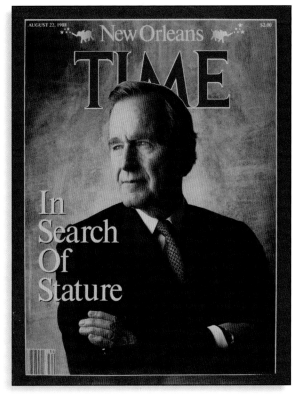

In Search of
Stature. Time
Magazine, 1988.
$3-4

Bush-Quayle 88. Bumper sticker. 1988. $3-4

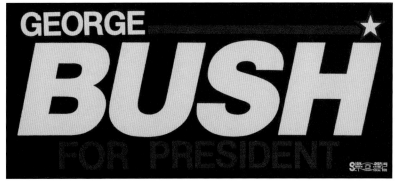

Bush For President, Bumper sticker. 1988. $3-4

Ronald Reagan and Vice President Bush. Mike Roberts Productions
postcard. 1980s. $10-12

Vice President
takes oath of office.
Coral-Lee postcard.
1980s. $2-3

George H.W. Bush

Mrs. George Bush. Republican Dinner
Ticket. 1988. $2-3

Saturday Night Live. Postcard of Bush imitation.
1992. $3-4

Dog Days. *Newsweek* magazine, 1992.
$3-4

The Commander In Chief. Desert Storm card from Topps. 1992. $4-5

William J. Clinton

President 1993 - 2001

William Jefferson Clinton was America's first Baby Boomer President of the United States.

Clinton was born on August 19, 1946 at a time when World War II had barely ended and the Cold War had barely begun.

The person who would eventually be the 42nd president of the U.S. was born in Hope, Arkansas. The family name on the day of Clinton's birth was Blythe. However three months after he was born his father died in a traffic accident. Four years later his mother married Roger Clinton and Clinton became the full family name.

Accounts say young Clinton was an excellent student in school and an excellent saxophone player as well. While in high school he became a delegate to Boy's Nation which in turn led to an inspiring meeting in the White House with President John F. Kennedy.

After graduating from Georgetown University the future president became a Rhodes Scholar in1968 and studied at Oxford University. By 1973 Clinton had acquired a law degree from Yale University.

Back once again in Arkansas an eager Clinton turned to politics. In 1974 he lost a campaign for U.S. Congress. The following year he married Hillary Rodham, and two years after his first political lost he was elected Arkansas Attorney General. In 1978 he was elected governor of that southern state, and four years later he was rejected by the voters of Arkansas. After yet another four-year wait he was again elected as governor.

A year before the 1988 presidential election Clinton seemed a highly unlikely but sometimes mentioned choice for the Democrat Party's nomination. Still unexpected things happened. Front-runner Senator Gary Hart withdrew after being accused of having an affair outside his marriage, and popular New York Governor Mario Cuomo declined an opportunity to run. Clinton too ultimately decided not to seek the presidency. Instead he nominated Massachusetts Governor Michael Dukakis at the Democratic National Convention.

Dukakis lost convincingly that presidential election year to Republican contender George H. W. Bush.

Four years later Clinton entered the 1992 presidential primaries with little impact. He finished third in Iowa and then finished a distant second in New Hampshire. Undaunted he labeled himself the "Comeback Kid" and went on to win a string of other primary elections and finally the nomination. Clinton next moved to the national election where he defeated both incumbent President George H. W. Bush and billionaire H. Ross Perot in November.

"Our democracy must be not only the envy of the world but the engine of our renewal," Clint declared at his inauguration. "There is nothing wrong with America than cannot be cured by what is right about America."

Upon taking office in the White House he became the third youngest President in history. The only younger two were Theodore Roosevelt and John Kennedy. Ultimately he would also be the first Democratic president since Franklin D. Roosevelt to win a second term.

Clinton had his share of successes during his White House years. The rate of unemployment fell to its lowest rate in modern history, while inflation also skirted its lowest rate in three decades. Crime rates declined and home ownership rose.

At the same time his extensive program of health care reform was a huge failure, and his North American Free Trade Agreement was highly controversial. Further, on his 'watch' the opposition Republican Party took control of the House of Representatives for the first time in 40 years.

Clinton won a second term of office in 1996 with a victory both over Republican Senator Robert Dole and return Reform candidate Ross Perot.

Military conflict erupted under Clinton's command in Somalia, in the Yugoslavian province of Kosovo, and in the Operation Desert Fox four-day bombing of Iran.

All of those varied things and a Federal budget surplus not withstanding, the Clinton administration was rocked with scandal after the president's affair with a 22-year-old White House intern. Charged with lying about his relationship under oath, the U.S. House voted to impeach President Clinton in 1998. The only other American president to be so impeached was President Andrew Johnson who was in office during the post Civil War years of the 19th century.

Early in 1999 after a trial lasting 21 days all counts of impeachment failed to get the required two-thirds majority in United States Senate. President Clinton remained president for the reminder of his term.

Later, President Clinton's wife, Hillary Rodham Clinton, became a U.S. Senator from New York, and still later was a candidate for President of the United States.

Presidential Sites:

Clinton Center & Birthplace, Hope, Arkansas, 870-777-4455

William J. Clinton Presidential Center, Little Rock, Arkansas, 501-370-8000

William J. Clinton

Fighting for the Forgotten Middle Class. Clinton
campaign brochure. 1992. $2-3

Golf scene. Silberne Sales postcard.
1990s. $3-4

Arkansas, The Home of William J. Clinton. Jenkins Enterprises
postcard, 1990s. $2-3

President Bill Clinton. Book & Tackle postcard. 1996.
$2-3

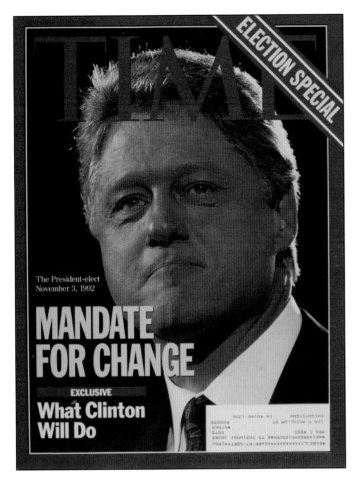

Mandate For Change. *Time* magazine, 1992. $3-4

The Hillary Factor. *Time* magazine. 1992. $3-4

President of the United States. Arkansas Post Card Company
postcard, 1992. $2-3

137 *William J. Clinton*

George W. Bush

President 2001 - 2009

George Walker Bush was the first president of America's 21st century.

In becoming the 43rd president of the United States he became the second son of an American president to hold office in the White House.

Ironically in the tempestuous terms of the presidency President Bush received some of the highest and lowest domestic approval ratings of American presidents in history.

The future president was born July 6, 1946 in New Haven, Connecticut.

Young Bush obtained a history degree from Yale University in 1968. Shortly afterwards he joined the Texas Air National Guard where he learned to fly the F-102 aircraft. He completed his service in the Guard in 1973 and two years later completed a master's degree in Business Administration.

After embarking on a career in the oil business, Bush married the love of his live Laura Welch Bush, a Texas school teacher and a librarian. While perhaps 'lucky' in love Bush was not so lucky in his first venture into politics. He lost a campaign to be elected a member of the U.S. Congress.

Business was booming however for Bush in the 1980s and in 1989 he and a group of partners purchased the franchise for the Texas Rangers professional baseball team. Bush again tried his hand at elected office in 1994 when he ran for governor of Texas. He defeated incumbent Ann Richards that year, and won re-election four years later.

Serving as 46th governor of Texas however was not his last stop toward the elective top. After six years as governor Bush launched a presidential campaign in the year 2000. He surpassed a crowded field to win the Republican presidential nomination. He campaigned that year with national slogans such as "compassionate conservative" and "prosperity with a purpose."

The national presidential election of 2000 was one of the most dramatic in American history.

Bush lost the popular vote by nearly a half a million votes, but appeared to win a majority in the electoral collage. While the entire population waited and watched the United States Supreme Court reversed the ruling of a Florida Supreme Court which had earlier ordered a recount of some 170,000 so-called "under votes". The lower court indicated these "under votes" involved ballots which had either registered a 'no' vote for the president or had registered a double vote for a presidential candidate. The high court ruled the recount would cease.

When George Walker Bush took the oath of office in Washington he held the same office that his father, George Herbert Walker Bush, had held. The only other father-son team had occurred centuries earlier with John Adams and John Quincy Adams.

On the morning of September 11, 2001 some eight months after President Bush took office terrorists attacked the World Trade Center in New York City and the Pentagon in Washington, D.C. Thousands of lives were lost.

That evening Bush addressed the nation from the Oval Office promising a strong response to the attacks. The president also stressed the need for the Nation to come together and offer comfort to the victims of the attacks. Just three days later Bush visited Ground Zero in New York where he addressed the fire fighters, police officers, and volunteers. Standing on a pile of rubble Bush delivered his message using a megaphone.

As a result of the 911 attacks Bush announced a global War on Terrorism. Ultimately it involved the invasion of Afghanistan that same year, and an invasion of Iraq two years later in 2003.

The wars were still underway when George W. Bush's term ended on January 20 of 2009. The president returned to his ranch in Tyler, Texas and a home he had retained there during his White House years.

Besides First Lady Laura Bush, other members of the Bush family included twin daughters Barbara Pierce Bush and Jenna Welch Hager. Family pets have included two dogs, Barney and Miss Beazley, plus Willie, the cat.

We're Gooder! Anti-Bush postcard-bumper sticker. 2004. $2-3

Laura Bush's Cowboy Cookies. WesternWhiteHouseGifts.com postcard, early 2000s. $3-4

President George W. Bush. Photo postcard from official portrait. 2001. $3-4

President Bush and Vladimir Putin. Slovakia Summit postcard. $4-5

George W. Bush

Barack Obama

President 2009 -

The 44th president, Barack Obama Jr., was the first president of the United States of America to be born in the 1960's decade. He was also the first African-American president of the United States, and the first to be born in the state of Hawaii.

President Obama was born August 4, 1961 in Honolulu, Hawaii.

The president's father, Obama Sr., was born and raised in a small village in the African country of Kenya where he grew up raising goats. The president's mother, Ann Dunham, grew up in a small town in Kansas.

The same year that Barack Obama was born, President John Kennedy spoke to the nation in his inaugural address. Part of the message was:

"To those people in the huts and villages of half the globe struggling to break the bonds of mass misery, we pledge our best efforts to help them help themselves, for whatever period is required. If a free society cannot help the many people who are poor, it cannot save the few that are rich."

Decades later, Obama would quote that speech and respond in his book *The Audacity of Hope* by noting:

"We will have to align our policies to help reduce the spheres of insecurity, poverty, and violence around the world, and give more people a stake in the global order that has served us well."

Both of Obama's parents were students at the University of Hawaii. She was a student and he was attending on a scholarship. Eventually the couple was divorced and Obama's father returned to Kenya while Barack grew up with his mother in Hawaii, and later in Indonesia. After a time, Obama moved back to Hawaii and lived with his grandparents.

As a young man, the future president moved to New York City and enrolled in Columbia University. He graduated in 1983.

After graduation, Obama moved to Chicago where he became a community organizer with a church-based group. The group's efforts were aimed at improving the living conditions of the poor. Ultimately Obama was accepted in Harvard Law School and obtained his law degree in 1991. He returned to Chicago to become a civil rights lawyer and to teach constitutional law.

Obama took a turn at politics and consequently served eight years in the Illinois State Senate. Moving on from there he launched a campaign to become a United States Senator from Illinois in 2004. It was successful capturing 70 percent of the vote. He became the third African-American since Reconstruction to be elected to the U.S. Senate.

In 2006 Obama authored *The Audacity of Hope.* Like his previous book, *Dreams from My Father*, *Audacity* became a best-seller. Since that time *Audacity* has been on *The New York Times* Best Seller list.

On February 10 of 2007, Obama announced his bid for the presidency from a site in Springfield, Illinois. After a long series of divisive primary elections with Senator Hillary Clinton, he was nominated by the Democratic Party at their national convention in August of 2008. At the time he selected Senator Joseph Biden of Delaware as his running mate.

In November of 2008 Obama won the presidency by defeating Republican John McCain. Obama captured more than 360 electoral votes and nearly 52 percent of the popular vote. A record 71 million viewers watched the results that evening on television.

That evening President-elect Obama spoke to masses of supporters in Chicago and to the nation:

"If there is anyone out there who still doubts that America is a place where all things are possible, who still wonders if the dream of our founders is alive in our time, who still questions the power of democracy, tonight is your answer."

He added:

"There will be setbacks and false starts. There are many who won't agree with every decision or policy I make as President, and we know that government can't solve every problem. But I will always be honest with you about the challenges we face. I will listen to you, especially when we disagree. And above all, I will ask you to join in the work of remaking this nation the only way its been done in America for two hundred and twenty-two years—block by block, brick by brick, calloused hand by calloused hand."

Barack Obama became a resident of the White House on January 20, 2009. He was joined by First Lady Michelle Robinson Obama and their two daughters, Malia and Sasha.

America Needs Obama. Bumper sticker. 2008. $2-3

Obama '08. www.wierdcards.blogspot.com postcard. 2008.

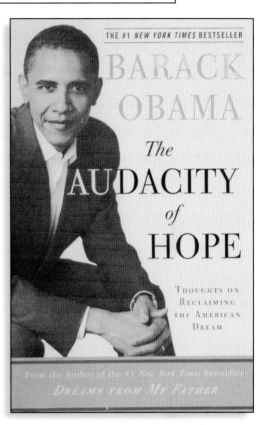

The Audacity of Hope by Barack Obama, 2006. $5-6

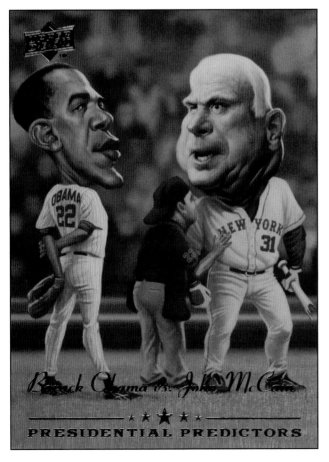

Barack Obama and John McCain. Presidential Predictions card from Upper Deck. 2008. $3-5

Vote For Change. www.wierdcards. blogspot.com postcard. 2008.

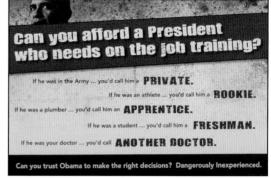

The Experience....? Anti-Obama
campaign postcard. 2008

They Agree.
Obama
campaign
postcard. 2008

Change We Can
Depend On. Obama
campaign postcard.
2008

History. *Indianapolis Star*
newspaper, Nov. 5, 2008

Bibliography

Durant, John and Alice. *Pictorial History of American Presidents*. New York, New York: A. S. Barnes and Company, 1958.

Furman, Bess. *White House Profile*. Indianapolis, Indiana: The Bobbs-Merrill Company, 1951.

Freidel, Frank. *Our Country's Presidents*. Washington, D.C.: National Geographic Society, 1966.

Frey, Marc and Todd Davis. *The New Big Book of U.S. Presidents*. Philadelphia, Pennsylvania: Courage Books, 2000.

Paletta, Lu Ann and Fred L. Worth. *The World Almanac Of Presidential Facts*. New York, New York: World Almanac, 1988.

Kane, Joseph. *Facts About The Presidents*. New York, New York: H.W. Wilson Company, 1959.

Sibert, Jacquelyn. *The Presidents*. Indianapolis, Indiana: Curtis Publishing Company, 1993.

Skarmeas, Nancy. *Our Presidents, Their Lives And Stories*. Nashville, Tennessee. Ideals Publication, 2004.

Sullivan, George. *Mr. President, A Book of U.S. Presidents*. New York, New York. Scholastic Inc., 1989.

INDEX